The Worship Problem

A Story of Surrender and Sacrifice

By Chuck Hooten

Chuck Hooten's books may be purchased for educational, business, or sales promotional use. For information, please contact Chuck Hooten, Peque Press, email chuckhooten@me.com, or visit www.chuckhooten.com.

Printed in the United States of America
Library of Congress Cataloging-in-Publication Data
Library of Congress Control Number:
FIRST EDITION
Chuck Hooten – 1st ed.
TITLE: The Worship Problem: A Story of Surrender and Sacrifice

Paperback ISBN: 978-1-7354423-0-3
1. RELIGION   2. SPIRITUALITY

Distributed by Peque Press

For Emily, Lily, Ava, Mae, and Josie—five amazing women God has given me to travel through life alongside. I love you. Thank you for pointing me to Jesus.

CONTENTS

Foreword

In late 2012, my wife and I made the 100-mile drive to Chattanooga, Tennessee, for a semi-blind double date of sorts. The purpose wasn't really for recreation but rather for dreaming God-sized dreams and considering his plan for each of our lives.

In this place we reconnected with an old friend who'd moved away, fallen in love, and married a worship leader from Birmingham. I'd heard a lot about this guy, Chuck, who was now sitting in front of me over lunch. He had charisma, good looks, and intelligence, yet that wasn't what really stood out. None of that was what we were looking for. It wasn't what we needed. It wasn't what could change lives.

We were looking for someone with complete dependence on Jesus—who was only interested in making his name great—and that was what I began to see in front of me.

Over the next few hours, I'm sure I spoke far too much and far too excitedly. But I couldn't contain my passion for what God was birthing in our new church. Candidly, we had no business talking to a guy like him for a role like ours. He'd served at great churches, led for incredible events, and written beautiful music. I, however, had a budding congregation with no staff, a thin budget, and a pocketful of aspirations that hadn't even come close to becoming reality.

We spent hours talking, laughing, and even crying over some of our past experiences in ministry. Ministry can be taxing. But even more concerning, we both knew it can be deceptive. Local church ministry has taken different shapes over the years and trends seemingly abound. Many should be embraced and others should not. Somewhere between lunch and our ice cream dessert, a few of these things came up in conversation.

Chuck began to gently articulate his concern with the celebrity culture that had emerged in the larger church, especially among worship leaders. Here was a guy who embraced new music and worship practices but also feared losing sight of some of the great traditions of the church that had come before us. I heard a guy who wanted to serve the church but wasn't willing to lose his family along the way. And, most notably, I heard a guy who felt the weight and responsibility associated with proclaiming the gospel of Jesus with clarity and personal conviction.

Years later, a lot of things have changed. Our church has grown exponentially. Serving together, we've seen lives transformed. We've started new things and we've stopped some older things. Openly, I used to cringe when people suggested that we've changed over the years. But the truth is that we have. We certainly don't look quite the same personally. Nor do we look quite the same corporately. Our own families have changed in unique and sweet ways. And so has our church family. God has not changed, however, nor has our desire to do what we say each and every Sunday: "not to lift up the name of any person on this stage or platform but exclusively the name of Christ."

At the heart of it all, there is worship.

The idea of worship has drawn you to this book. If worship didn't matter to you, you wouldn't have even made it these few pages in. You'll soon read where Chuck addresses what worship really is and how it should be defined. And you can be assured that Jesus is at the center of it all.

In this book, you won't find any prescriptive steps for being a good worship leader. Nor will you find a tutorial on how to create perfect harmonies or a spectacular event. But you will be drawn toward what it means to truly worship. And you'll become a better worshipper. And that's because you'll better know this God that we're worshipping. Quite simply, we cannot give away that which we do not have. We cannot teach that which we don't understand. And we cannot share that which we haven't experienced.

My prayer for you would be that of Ephesians 3:16-19, "that according to the riches of his glory he may grant you to be strengthened with power through his Spirit in your inner being, so that Christ may dwell in your hearts through faith—that you, being rooted and grounded in love, may have strength to comprehend with all the saints what is the breadth and length and height and depth, and to know the love of Christ that surpasses knowledge, that you may be filled with all the fullness of God."

I still look back at that lunch in Chattanooga with great fondness. We each had stories to share, and we both desired to be part of something that demanded an utter dependence upon the Father. And more personally, I gained a dear friend that day—a brother who has continually reminded our church to exclusively lift up the name of Jesus. I also gained a co-laborer whom I can still trust today has the glory of God and the expansion of the kingdom as his highest priority.

Our friendship has made me a better man, a better husband, a better father, and a better pastor. And it's certainly made me a better worshipper. I occasionally reflect on how our trajectory changed because of that lunch. Unfortunately, I doubt Chuck will be able to join each of you for lunch in the coming days. However, in this book, you will absolutely find the very same Jesus that has been transforming our lives and our worship all these years. Pull up a chair and get to know this Jesus. It will change your life, and it will undoubtedly change your worship!

Jason Hayes
Lead Pastor
Shoreline Church

Introduction

When I was six years old, my family lived with my Aunt Caroline and Uncle Fred for a little while. My parents had liquidated belongings and habitation in preparation for a move to Texas, where my dad would attend seminary. As we bunked with family, life went on as regularly as it could.

A beautiful cherry tree stood in the front yard of their house. It bloomed and wilted with clockwork regularity, signaling the changing of seasons. It smelled amazing in the spring and provided shade in the summer. It was my favorite place to play. One afternoon I decided to make the long climb to the top. My brother, who was five at the time, craned his neck to watch me make my glorious ascent into the tree's canopy.

My sudden descent felt like an eternity. I don't remember much about being six, but I remember that fall. I bumped and bounced through the spiderweb pattern of cherry tree branches until I finally hit the ground with a dull thud. To brace myself for impact, I reached my short arms behind me, letting my hands hit the ground first. Six-year-old wrists aren't made to withstand the effects of a fall that great. They both broke instantly. I felt them crack.

I spent the next few weeks wearing giant plaster casts on both arms. Everywhere I went, I was a danger to humanity. A six-year-old with two casts is a battering ram of accidental destruction. At the school book fair, I turned around too quickly and hit a kid in the head. I left scratches all over Aunt Caroline's furniture from just sitting and resting my arms. My broken arms affected everything and everyone around me.

In this book, we will see how humanity's story started at a tree and was altered forever by a terrible fall. The impact of that fall didn't result in broken bones set by plaster casts; it broke the parts of us that were meant to connect with our creator. We will see that our problem since that day has been one of false worship. Just like plaster casts on wooden furniture, our false worship has damaged and affected everything around us. Nothing has remained untouched by our brokenness. We have become battering rams of destruction as we have thrown off the worship we were created for, replacing it with devotion of our own design.

I am excited to share this book with you. My journey in worship leadership has been long and ever-changing. I began leading worship in 1994 at the age of sixteen. That year I received a guitar for Christmas, and with three chords and a willingness to serve, I jumped into leading the worship band at my youth group. I never stopped serving and have been leading worship in the church for more than twenty years.

Much has changed in those twenty years. The worship genre of music has taken off like a rocket. Twenty-somethings in skinny jeans have replaced older men in suits, and bands, albums, and concerts are the worship language of our day. Some of this shift is good, providing new and fresh language for the church to express its devotion to the divine. Some of it, however, has moved the church down a dangerous road that focuses on form rather than the heartbeat of what worship truly is.

My hope for this book is that we would be reminded that worship is not singing songs. Worship is not beautiful music played in a darkened room. Worship is not even just saying the right things about God to the ingredients of rhythm and melody. While all of these things can be responses of a worshipper, these things alone mean nothing apart from a life marked by surrender and sacrifice.

The story of the Old Testament reveals this reality with stunning clarity. I pray that as you read the story of God and his people in the Old Testament, you are reminded who you were created to be and that your life is gloriously altered. That the broken bones of false worship in your life are set straight and made whole. That you can once again run and play under the tree in the garden, side by side with your creator.

Chapter 1

The Worship Problem

We have a worship problem. It is the problem that gives birth to and drives all of the other problems in our lives. Countless volumes have been written on how to scratch the itch, fix the issue, or fill the void that seems to beset us and pull us backward, and yet here we are, just like we have always been—the same. We are hardwired from birth to act and function in a way that will bring us pain and then to try and find solutions to that pain with things that make the problem worse. We are like a soldier with a bullet wound in the leg, trying to make the pain go away by shooting the other leg with a different gun. This is who we are. But it is not who we have always been.

Why are we like this? What is the root of all of this hurt? It goes back much further than you might imagine—further than your birth, even further than your immediate family history. While some of us may have stories of neglect and abuse that have fueled and pushed us toward pain, these factors alone cannot take credit for the depth of our brokenness. Our problems and hurts can be traced back to the earliest roots of our family tree, to a place where we lived so long ago, in a garden called Eden. Our problem is a worship problem at its core.

Back so long ago in Eden, we were created to worship in a specific way, in submission to a specific God, to live in the perfection we were meant to enjoy. In our desire to define worship and its focus, we lost ourselves and the real object of our worship completely. Our decision to redefine worship started the snowball of every broken story that would be told from then until now, yours and mine included.

Our stories are different and stretch across a multiplicity of crazy twists and turns. We are from different races, countries, socioeconomic brackets, and genders. We hold up our uniqueness as badges of honor, trying to stand out from the normalcy of life and humanness. And yet, at the root of everything, we are the same. Spoiled fruit, fallen from the same tree. As meandering as our stories appear, they all go back to one fatal moment—an incredible fall that stole from us the ability to be who we are. A moment that took from us the ability to truly worship as we were created to and robbed us of real life.

As a pastor who works with broken people all the time and who is painfully broken himself, I get a front-row seat as to how this works itself out daily.

Not long ago, I sat in my office with Jeff, a new friend in the faith, and once again saw the effects of the worship problem up close and personal. Jeff had been attending a class I was teaching on the Old Testament, and after the week where we studied some of the prophets, he emailed me and asked if we could talk. He told me that his heart was broken because he had abandoned his love for God and that his life was a story of isolation and depression. He asked if he could come and confess some things face-to-face.

His email began with an amazingly honest statement, taken from the Old Testament book of Hosea: "I am Gomer." What an intro!

God told the prophet Hosea to marry a prostitute named Gomer, a woman who would not be faithful to him as a wife. It is a heartbreaking story of unwavering faithfulness amid unfaithfulness. It is a summation of my story and yours. Because of his love, Hosea was devoted to his unfaithful bride, even repurchasing her from the slave traders to whom she found herself repeatedly indebted. Through Hosea, God showed the people of Israel how their hearts had turned from worship into the arms of other lovers. He demonstrated how far he was willing to go to make sure they would find their way back home again.

As we talked about the beautiful faithfulness of God, Jeff sat dumbfounded that anyone could love him that way after everything he had done. He had grown up in a church that taught God expected perfection to have his love. After becoming an adult, he had walked away from the faith because he realized that perfection was impossible. Walking away had led him to seek out help and healing in alcohol and the arms of other men. None of it brought what he had hoped it would. None of it ever does. As we sat in my office, both of us looking through hot tears, he spoke of shame because he had wasted sixty-five years chasing down solutions that hadn't brought relief. Jeff worried that he had consumed a lifetime giving his affection to other lovers, and he feared that God couldn't possibly love him anymore.

Jeff and I talked for two hours about the love of God and the worship problem. All of his loss and hurt, as well as mine, can be traced back to the issue of false worship and hearts broken by idols that haven't delivered what they promised. But God is faithful even when we are not. God is like Hosea. Jeff was learning that even after we have run again and again into the arms of false gods, the true God is always waiting to catch us when we return to him in surrender. No life is wasted that lands in the arms of God.

The return to true worship doesn't have an age limit or wrong choice restriction—the next moment can be the one where your life is changed forever. You will find everything you were meant to be and more when you finally realize that you were created to be a fully engaged worshipper of God. It is only when we move back into the rhythms of true worship that we will find what was lost so long ago.

In this book, we will start at the beginning, in Genesis, and work our way through the biblical story of worship lost and then found again. In the journey, you will see yourself as you see the nation of Israel struggle to return to a place of true worship. The worship problem is not easily solved. It cannot be remedied by anything that we can conjure up or do ourselves. As we long to have the worship problem assuaged within the darkness of our own lives, we will find that the only hope of redemption is found in God's desire for us to know him intimately. And that intimacy only comes through worship.

Chapter 2

What Worship Is

———

Before we jump into the story of worship in the Old Testament, it would be helpful to talk about the concept of worship itself. Much has been written over the ages about what worship is and is not. There are countless volumes committed to the task of clarifying the terms and definitions relating to the topic. My goal here is not to re-create the wheel on the subject of worship. But I do want to give a good working definition of what we are talking about so that we might identify how it went wrong and what will be required to fix it.

I will never forget my first trip to the Grand Canyon. A friend of mine was moving from Alabama to California, and I was part of the crew that drove him from Bama to Hollywood. En route, we decided that a slight detour to see a giant hole in the ground was warranted. As I stood at the edge, looking down at the enormity of the canyon, I was overwhelmed. My reaction to the sight was palpable—a mix of nervous and excited at the same time. It is terrifying to realize that if the wind blows too hard, you will fall a mile and die. Just like my reaction to the Grand Canyon was instant and overwhelming, the same is true about worship.

Worship is a reaction to the revelation of God.

Mark it down. Memorize it. In this simple idea, we find the key to understanding the mechanics of true worship.

It works like this. God reveals himself to a person or a group of people. Because of that revelation, there is a reaction, a response of surrender and sacrifice. What was lost in the past comes roaring back as we encounter God in the present. Our selfishness is replaced by selflessness, and our need for control is replaced by surrender. These are the bedrock reactions when we worship something.

One of my greatest childhood memories was when my dad surprised my brother and me with tickets to the first-ever SEC football championship game. It was a freezing night in Birmingham, Alabama, as we sat huddled in the end zone of Legion Field. We were excited though. Football history was in the making as the Alabama Crimson Tide and Florida Gators took the field.

As the game neared completion, it seemed like the Gators were going to win. The score was knotted at 21-21 with a little over three minutes left to play. The Gators were driving. Momentum was on their side. That was until the Tide's Antonio Langham stepped in front of a pass thrown by Gators quarterback Shane Matthews and returned it for a game-winning touchdown. Langham ran it right into the end zone where we were sitting. I'm pretty sure he pointed at me. I have never heard a louder roar out of a group of people than when he intercepted that ball. It was electric.

It was worship.

I like football. I like baseball. I like basketball. I pretty much like it all. In my town, sports are a massive source of worship for individuals and families. Those pulling for their favorite sports team surrender their undying allegiance to the men and women who run around on the field or the court, while at the same time sacrificing large amounts of time and resources to see them play. They respond to the teams with loud sounds of worship and praise. These responses reveal the objects of our worship. By looking at what provokes our reaction of surrender and sacrifice, we come to understand where our devotion lies.

The same is true when we think about the worship of God. Worship has never been just simply saying or singing the right things about God. It is not expressed by showing up to a room to sing a few songs a couple of times a month. In worship, God is not prepping us for a test about who he is that we take when we die. There is no heavenly entrance exam like college or grad school. Facts about God that do not elicit responses of surrender and sacrifice are only cold facts; they are not worship.

A true worshipper is someone who has seen God through the revelation of the Holy Spirit. Someone who has changed from a person marked by selfishness to a person of surrender and sacrifice. Someone who has been altered to resonate and reflect the image of God through the way they live day to day. Worship is not saying true things; it is becoming true things. The difficulty is that it requires us to surrender everything. To not surrender all is to miss God altogether.

Worship without surrender is idolatry. This is the theme of Israel's story. They longed to worship God, but on their terms, surrounded by the things that they loved and cherished. They demanded that God surrender to their will as they disregarded his altogether. As we read about them, we will be presented with a picture of ourselves. Worship of God requires a shift in who we are and what we love. It will always cause change.

There are two competing narratives at play in our lives that become crystal clear as we have a revelation of God. There is the story that we seek to write for ourselves and the one God wants to write for us. Worship is found in the tension between those two spaces. Both cannot be true together. Will we become people who surrender to the will and work of God in our lives, or will we maintain autonomy and tell our own story instead? As we walk through the Old Testament, we will find that the answer to this question will be the source of Israel's idolatry and undoing.

Are you being changed? Through Jesus, are you accepting the invitation to come into the presence of God to be made into his image, or are you looking from afar, remaking him into your own? Those who genuinely seek to worship the divine are altered and pressed into his holiness. Those who do not will remain the same. If we refuse this change, the worship problem will continue in perpetuity, resulting in futility and eternal death. Those who are willing to come into the presence of God through worship will be made into something new. They will be altered into who they were always meant to be, living on through eternal life.

We all know people who can share stories of how this reality has changed their lives. Who they were melted in the light of how God has transformed them. It makes me think of my friend T. K.

T. K. has struggled with addiction to drugs and alcohol since high school. There are lots of reasons for this reality, but he will tell you that his real issue was that he had a worship problem. He used to be the center of his universe. When pain and loss began to creep in, his reaction was to control and medicate. He let drug use become the balm that brought relief.

I was the first from our church to arrive at the hospital after T. K. overdosed for the second time that year. While alone at home, he had taken a drug, and he knew in an instant that he had taken too much. He said the only thing that ran through his mind was, "Oh no, I'm dead." By all accounts, he should have been. But he survived. The overdose happened on one of the coldest nights of the year. In his depressed stupor, he had forgotten to turn on the heat in his house. The doctor said T. K.'s home was so cold that it limited the swelling in his brain, keeping him alive. God had more for T. K.

When he woke up, we talked about the whys and whats of his overdose, but what we talked about the most was the fact that God loved him. God was still calling and inviting him to become what he was always created to be—a true worshipper of God. T. K. embraced the call and started on a journey toward surrender and sacrifice. His worship is now beautiful. He currently leads worship and speaks about addiction to others who have the same worship issue. The change is stark. The joy in his life is palpable. He is a walking and breathing dispenser of the fruits of the Holy Spirit mentioned in Galatians 5:22. T. K. is overcome by the revelation of God and has reacted with surrender and sacrifice. He has kneeled in worship. He is changed.

This surrender is what we are talking about when we speak of worship. We are never referring to lights and loud music in a darkened room. We are referring to those who have been invited into the presence of God. Invited into the sanctuary. Invited to commune with him through surrender and sacrifice.

The story of the Bible begins with this reality as the norm. The story begins in a garden, in a sanctuary of worship, in a special place called Eden. As we start with worship in the beginning and move into the broken worship of the Old Testament, I pray that we see how our worship problem might be solved in the present.

Chapter 3

Worship in the Beginning

————————

Right at the start of the Bible, contained within the poetry of the first three verses of Genesis, we see the entire story of what will follow for the rest of history.

God speaks into chaos and turns what was without form and void into something filled with purpose. God says, "Let there be light," and the dark shines in obedience to his creative power. God speaks to nothingness, and in an instant, it becomes somethingness because it is subject to the speech of God. The story of creation is the blueprint of how God will solve our worship problem in the future. By his word, things that are broken will be set straight again. His word will bring the lost back home.

The creation account reverberates with the voice of God, bringing into being a world full of things that can only be described as good. Nothing is out of place, no leaf is where it doesn't belong, no cloud moves outside of the shape that will bring the most declarative glory to the one who spoke it into being. The world is perfect, and contained within its glorious perfection, we find a man and a woman, living in a garden.

Gardens are amazing places. They are meant to be places of growth, life, and beauty. Within carefully crafted rows, seeds germinate and spring to life in forms that bear all kinds of textures, colors, and flavors to beautify and sustain the world. My great-grandmother, Mama Castleberry, was a master gardener. Her house was full of jars bearing the fruits of her continuous labor. You could taste and see that the garden life was a good one. This and so much more points to the reason why Adam and Eve were meant to live in such a place.

As we think about worship, it is essential to understand what the Garden of Eden was and what it represented. The Garden of Eden was a specific place within the creation itself, standing out as unique amid every place God had formed by his speech. The Garden was much more than merely the site where God placed Adam and Eve to live. It wasn't just a great vacation home. The Garden was where Adam and Eve communed with the divine. There they grew in deep relationship with God and one another. They sprouted and flourished in the light of his glory and goodness. God met Adam and Eve face-to-face. He walked with them as one walks with a friend or family member, speaking long and slow of who they were and where they were going.

As we read the creation account, it becomes evident the Garden of Eden was a sanctuary. More specifically, it was a place of worship. Amid the vastness of creation, it was the place where heaven and earth came together and overlapped as one.

Hold your hands out in front of you. Two separate hands, distinct in time and space. Now interlock your fingers. The space where your hands come together is what a sanctuary does. A sanctuary is the connecting space between two distinct places. God has always sought to create spaces where this is reality. His desire in creation is to be near us. To have a special place where our lives and world mesh with his. A place of communion between heaven and earth. A space where the spirit of God can rest. The Garden of Eden fit this bill in every way.

Here is the crazy reality in the present for those who are in Christ: We are the new sanctuary, the new Eden. The church has become the place where heaven and earth come together as one. We are the new temple where the spirit of God wants to live. Like a garden, our lives now bear the potential for growth and life springing from the spirit of God. Paul puts it like this:

Or do you not know that your body is a temple of the Holy Spirit within you, whom you have from God? You are not your own, for you were bought with a price. So glorify God in your body. (1 Corinthians 6:19–20)

This is why fixing the worship problem is vital. God wants to use you as a means to connect a broken world back to himself. As the special place where heaven and earth come together, you are now the conduit for another person to meet God. When someone speaks with you, they are meant to get a sense of the divine. A touch from your hand is meant to be a touch from Jesus himself.

Paul says later in the book of 1 Corinthians that the church has become the "body of Christ." We are his hands, feet, and eyes in the world. We will talk about this later as we look at the temple of Solomon, but know that as you read about Eden, you learn what God desires to do in you through worship. He wants you to grow. To spring with life and beauty. He wants to walk among his people, and he wants to use you to do it.

I hope you have had the chance to be around people like this. People whose mere presence gives you a sense of what God is like. I have had the privilege of knowing many people who exude this quality. Mike Fox is one of them.

I met Mike years ago through random circumstances. I had just seen a documentary on the refugee crisis in Darfur. I was moved to find people who would help take the love of Jesus to children orphaned by war and other horrible situations created by the worship problem. A quick internet search brought me to a group called the Global Orphan Project. I shot Mike an email and introduced myself, not really expecting a reply. I was shocked when he personally called me later that same day. We have been friends ever since.

Mike's story of submission and sacrifice oozes with the beauty of worship. To speak and walk with him for five minutes is to see the kingdom of God connecting with the brokenness of earth. He has become the hands and feet of Jesus in flesh and blood. He is living proof of what can be done when people do more than give lip service to worship. People who give their whole lives in submission to the worship of God change the brokenness of the world.

Mike came face-to-face with the orphan crisis while on a mission trip to Cambodia. Moved by the great need, he came home and leveraged his interest in an oil and gas company to start the Global Orphan Project. In an instant, he was transformed from a successful businessman into a weapon against darkness. In the years since, millions of people all over the world have been impacted by the incredible work of this group. I could write pages on the stories of hope and redemption that have come through their work. I encourage you to look them up and join in.

This is God's heart for everyone. Not to sell companies and start ministries but to be willing to become people who orient their lives around the mission of bringing Jesus to those with whom we come in contact. We are called to connect heaven and earth through the Holy Spirit. This is what worship does. This is what submission and sacrifice produce. We are meant to be a temple, the place where heaven and earth collide. We are the return to Eden for a world that doesn't know the way.

Many of us have never experienced this depth in worship. We have jumped from one thing to another, looking for the next spiritual high through the next great song or album. Worship isn't contained in a feeling we get from hearing something—it is a response we live out as we are becoming something. We do not lack in worship because of the content on our playlists—we lack because we are not being changed into the temple we were meant to become. If the temple is lost, where will God's spirit rest?

The beauty of Eden was not to last. What stood as a shining place of beauty and life was demolished under the crushing darkness of rebellion and death. After Eden is lost, God will make other sanctuaries where his spirit can commune with creation. They will be shadows of the glory that had been found in Eden, but God's heart will always be to abide with his people in worship. Because of this, he will make new ways for us to enter into his presence. After the Fall, these places come in the form of temporary tents and temples made of cedar and stone. However, in the beginning, the perfect sanctuary was found in the Garden of Eden, and it was beautiful.

Eden weaves its way throughout the entire story of the Bible. Jesus used the imagery of a garden as he prayed the night before his trial and execution. After his death and burial, Mary Magdalene first encounters the resurrected Jesus in another garden.

Jesus said to her, "Woman, why are you weeping? Whom are you seeking?" Supposing him to be the gardener, she said to him, "Sir, if you have carried him away, tell me where you have laid him, and I will take him away." Jesus said to her, "Mary." She turned and said to him in Aramaic, "Rabboni!" (which means Teacher). (John 20:15–16)

Mary wasn't wrong. Jesus's mission had been to open the door back to the garden, back to the original sanctuary, where worship could be expressed and enjoyed in completion. As she fell into his resurrected arms, the heart of God burst with joy as well. Worship was re-created at last.

God's intention in creation has always been to commune with humankind in the sanctuary. We were made to be with God in the special place he has made for us to see him and know him intimately. The purpose of your existence is to know God and worship through the response of surrender and sacrifice. While many of us feel like God is angry or has run away and hidden himself, we will see as we go along that we are actually the ones who have done the hiding. God's heart is, and always has been, to be with his people through worship.

Eden is the starting point and serves as the blueprint for what God will restore. Perfection in the Garden is replaced by the worship problem that has plagued humanity ever since. But even when all seems lost, God has a plan to heal what we have broken.

Chapter 4

Where It All Went Wrong

Why did Adam and Eve eat the fruit? Kids ask this question all the time. I mean, if you had everything at your fingertips and were told not to do this one thing, why in the world would you risk everything for that one thing? If your mom said you could have an endless supply of junk food if you would agree not to eat her chocolate-covered chocolate with sprinkles, it seems like a no-brainer to take that deal. And yet, their story and our story is that everything was not enough. We wanted more.

In the center of the Garden stood a tree. God called it the tree of the knowledge of good and evil, but it was much more than just a plant with delicious fruit growing from its branches. The tree that stood in the center of the Garden was central to the worship Adam and Eve were created to enjoy. It represented surrender to the will of God. It was a means for Adam and Eve to place themselves in a posture of trust and obedience, to live the reality that they were not the ones who would decide what worship would be. True worship exists in this tension between autonomy and surrender to the story of God.

As we read of the Fall, we see that it was not the fruit itself that the serpent used to tempt Eve—it was what the fruit represented. Since God had created them for surrender, the serpent was going to tempt them with control.

Now the serpent was more crafty than any other beast of the field that the LORD God had made. He said to the woman, "Did God actually say, 'You shall not eat of any tree in the garden'?" And the woman said to the serpent, "We may eat of the fruit of the trees in the garden, but God said, 'You shall not eat of the fruit of the tree that is in the midst of the garden, neither shall you touch it, lest you die.'" But the serpent said to the woman, "You will not surely die. For God knows that when you eat of it your eyes will be opened, and you will be like God, knowing good and evil." (Genesis 3:1–5)

"Did God really say?" Notice that the serpent didn't question anything God had made. To look around the Garden of Eden was to see only perfection. God himself had said that all the things he had created shone with his goodness. There was no denying that reality. Because of this, the serpent questioned God's word, the things he had spoken.

The entire creation had been brought into existence by God's speech. In the beginning, God said, "Let there be light," and where there had been nothing, now there was light. The mark of God's creative power is that what he declares becomes reality. The speech of God—his word and declarative authority—was the center of the newly made creation. By his word, everything had found its being, and by his word, everything was being sustained.

Adam and Eve's part in worship was to surrender to the words of God, and now in the middle of perfection, the serpent was telling them that God's words couldn't be trusted. He said God was holding out on them, that God's story was limiting their potential. In essence, the serpent was whispering, "You would be a better storyteller than God. Why don't you take the pen out of his hand and write your own ending? If you do, you will become just like him."

The craziness of the serpent's assertions lies in the fact that Adam and Eve were already the most like God they could ever be. They were created in his image, and in their surrender to his word, they were revealing his perfect nature. The serpent was challenging God's command to live in surrender as if it were limiting their ability to express godliness and worship. The temptation to eat was one of autonomy and anarchy fueled by the desire to become like God.

God lives in surrender. Father, Son, and Spirit exist in perfect submission to one another. Surrender and sacrifice don't make us lose our connection with God—they provide us the means to understand and reflect him. Jesus demonstrates how surrender and sacrifice are linked to intimacy with God as he submits to the will of the Father on his way to the cross. When Jesus says in the garden of

Gethsemane, "Not my will but yours be done," he is no less God than when he was commanding the oceans into existence by his word. By his act of surrender in another garden, he is re-creating the worship that was destroyed by Adam and Eve's refusal to say the same.

In Eden, the very thing the serpent offered was something Eve already possessed. Eve wanted more, and the rest is tragic history. She listened to the serpent and believed his lies. Next, Adam listened to Eve, and what they thought would give them freedom and life brought death and placed them in chains. In one single act, they traded what they already had for the lie of something that didn't exist.

By listening to the serpent, Adam and Eve were altered forever, as was their worship. Like rotten fruit at the base of a tree, Adam and Eve's worship began to shrivel and die as the object of their sacrifice and surrender changed from God to themselves. No longer would the creative, powerful, and sustaining voice of God dictate what worship would be. Now the voice and mind of humanity would set the parameters for what was good and lovely.

The echoes of this reality reverberate to this day. Lesser gods who look and sound like us captivate our attention and steal our sacrifice and submission. One morning I was watching a show called *The World According to Jeff Goldblum*. I can never see Goldblum without picturing a giant T. rex and hearing the words, "Must go faster, must go faster," ringing in my ears. In this episode, he was exploring the sneaker industry and the world's fascination with and love of these particular shoes. He started the show with a trip to an event called Sneaker Con, a one-day extravaganza of everything sneakers. People from all over the world come to Sneaker Con to buy and sell shoes. Some sell for hundreds of dollars. Some for thousands. In a span of just a few hours, millions of dollars change hands at this event. The excitement of those in attendance is palpable. Goldblum is puzzled by such exuberance over a product made of rubber and fiber. He seems to think the whole thing is a little crazy.

I was struck by the question he asked at the start of the show because it cuts right to the core of what we are talking about. He equated Sneaker Con to a worship service and likened the attendees to the faithful. He asked, "What is the reason for this worship of sneakers?" It is a question with an answer that goes back to the beginning, back to the serpent and Eve and the Garden of Eden. Some of the sneaker faithful are willing to devote their entire lives to the pursuit of sneaker worship. They are eager to make sacrifices; they have submitted to the call.

When worship is reoriented around us, the things birthed out of our desires and the gods we create become trivial and dull. Millions of dollars and countless hours are devoted to cheering on men and women who hit, throw, and run around with a ball. We idolize people with talents we wish we had. *American Idol* is not tongue in cheek. Music, movies, and art contain multiple ways for us to sacrifice and worship at the feet of those who speak into the lostness we experience. They speak our language; they know our pain. We see them as priests who can lead us to places where we will feel whole again. We sacrifice to them our money; we surrender to them our time and affection.

Of course, the greatest idol is often the one that stares back at us in the mirror every morning. When the serpent whispered to Eve, "You will become like God," he was not wholly untruthful. What he failed to tell Adam and Eve is what terrible gods they would make.

Fashion, beauty, and self-promotion are multibillion-dollar industries all over the world. With the advent of social media, our desire to become gods has been ignited to a fever pitch. Notice me! See me! Like me! Love me! Our money is spent on things that will make us beautiful so that others will notice and bow down to the altar of the self. The wheel is endless because those we are seeking as our worshippers are simultaneously asking of us the same.

When Adam and Eve became the object of their own worship, everything terrible was unleashed on the world. Hearts that previously had only known love and unity were altered into dark places filled with mistrust and shame. Those who had shone with the image of God retreated into shadows because they saw themselves as ugly and exposed. Their response to "freedom" was to hide in the bushes from one another and from God. We are still hiding today.

While Adam and Eve hid in the bushes from shame, God came walking in the Garden in the cool of the day. He was looking for his friends in the sanctuary. It would be the last walk they would take together in that beautiful, sacred space. But even amid tragedy, God set events into motion to bring them back to Eden once again. He was sad they had to leave. Later, God told his people that his heart was to go back to that place where he could walk among them once again.

I will make my dwelling among you, and my soul shall not abhor you. And I will walk among you and will be your God, and you shall be my people. (Leviticus 26:11–12)

The "walk among you" part is a direct reference to the Garden of Eden. God's plan is to bring us back as well. It is hard to believe this is true—that God still longs to be near us through renewed worship. People tell me they are convinced that God wants nothing to do with them because of what they have done and what they have become. They are hiding from the only one who can fix what they have broken.

Several years ago, I was leading worship at an event hosted at Louisiana Tech University for students from all over the Southeast. At a break in between sessions, a high school girl walked by me and said hello with a shy smile. Before she could walk away, I started up a conversation and asked what her name was and where she was from. As we stood talking, I noticed the marks where she had taken razor blades to her wrists to cut trailways of pain into her arms.

"Tell me about these marks. What do they represent?" I asked quietly.

Her eyes dropped in shame. I had pointed out the symbol of everything she wanted to run away from. She cried as she told me about her father being killed in a car accident and a life marked by neglect and abuse from those who should have provided shelter and love. In her loneliness, she had tried everything at her disposal to make the pain go away. When none of those worked, she started cutting. She decided that if her pain would always be present, she could at least control some of it herself.

Beneath her shame, loss, and pain was a deeper issue. She stated with certainty that all the Jesus stuff we had been singing and speaking about couldn't be for her.

"I've strayed too far and done too much for God to love me anymore," she said.

As she stood there and cried, I started crying as well. "Not only does God want to be with you," I said, "the story of the Bible is also his plan to make it possible for you to be with him, scars and all."

The good news of Jesus was not that God was so angry that she better straighten up or else. Instead, it was that God so loved the world that he gave his son. For sinners. For me. For her. For you.

One of the greatest mysteries in the universe is the answer to why this is true. Why would God want to walk with me? Why would God work so hard to provide a way for me to return to the worship of the Garden of Eden? I offer nothing that he doesn't already possess. If God wants to elevate his street cred, I am the last person he should want walking alongside him, and yet he has called us to do just that. God not only wants to be with me, he also wants to live within me.

Adam and Eve were forced to leave Eden. They weren't fit to remain in the sanctuary any longer. Only those who look like God can be in the presence of God, and Adam and Eve had chosen themselves over the image they were crafted to bear. The scene and tone of God's broken heart can be felt as he speaks to them.

Earlier God had seen the beauty of what he had done and said it was good. As the carnage of the Fall begins to manifest, God's question for Adam and Eve points to something different as he asks them, "What have you done?" The speech of God had brought life. Adam and Eve's speech was now bringing death. When God saw what he had done, it was good; when God saw what we had done, his heart broke at the disarray and chaos. God's words had brought light from darkness; our words took us from the light back into the dark.

God begins speaking differently. Curses are brought against those who have rebelled. Adam, Eve, and the serpent fall under this new form of speech. Even the ground is cursed, unable to escape the curse of sin. What was once described as good had now fallen under the weight of humanity's destructive storytelling. But amid this chaos, shining like a shaft of light in the ensuing dark, God speaks a word that stands out among the curses. He speaks a promise that starts as a whisper but ends in a resounding storm of love and power. God says to the serpent and to Eve:

"I will put enmity between you and the woman, and between your offspring and her offspring; he shall bruise your head, and you shall bruise his heel." (Genesis 3:15)

If this verse sounds mysterious and coded, don't worry, it did to them as well. God is saying that he would do something to rectify what had been broken. Eve would have a son in her lineage who would do battle with the evil serpent. The serpent would bite the son, but the son would deliver a death blow to the serpent's head. God took upon himself the responsibility of fixing what had been broken. Worship would not be renewed and restored by the work of Adam and Eve. It would take the action and continued speech of God himself to remake what had been undone.

The start of John's gospel resounds with the hope of the promise made in Genesis 3. God will never stop speaking, and he will always follow through on what he has said he would do. The first chapter of John reads like a restatement of Genesis 1, with one fantastic difference. This time God doesn't just speak into the darkness—he enters the darkness himself. The Word of God, the story of God, the speech of God comes to life. God steps into our world in living color. The offspring of Eve is named Jesus, and he will go to battle against the serpent of old to restore the worship that was lost. God will again say, "Let there be light," but he will do it wearing flesh and bones.

In the beginning was the Word, and the Word was with God, and the Word was God. He was in the beginning with God. All things were made through him, and without him was not any thing made that was made. In him was life, and the life was the light of men. The light shines in the darkness, and the darkness has not overcome it. (John 1:1–5)

Jesus will restore what was lost in the Garden. He will be the one to open the way for us to worship once again in the presence of God. Since the beginning, this has been the plan. He has always wanted us to go back to the Garden, back to true worship. We will say more about this later, but know the hopelessness of the Fall should always be tempered with the promise of what is to come. God will not leave us on the outside of his presence. Even though our choice was to abandon his love, his choice will always be to lavish us with his.

Because Adam and Eve were created for worship, the loss of Eden was devastating. Access to the sanctuary was gone. Like a tree removed from the life-giving properties of the soil, when humankind is forced from the presence of God, they began to shrivel and die, physically and spiritually. It didn't take long for the new parameters of worship to show up in horrible ways. Worship had been broken and changed.

Chapter 5

Worship After the Fall

Worship in Eden was a picture of humanity submitting to the will and voice of God. Worship and deep fellowship with the divine were the result. As we saw in the last chapter, what followed the Fall was the reversal of perfection. Fellowship and community were shattered between God and his creation as worship was ruined by sin.

In the Garden, God commanded Adam to rule over creation, name the animals, and serve as a priest in the sanctuary of Eden. After the Fall, Adam lost this purpose as the ground was cursed, producing thorns that thwarted God's original desire for Adam to rule over and control it. The communion and fellowship between humankind were also altered and broken in horrible ways. After their sin, the man and woman realized they were naked, a picture of shame and loss of vulnerability. Before the Fall, they had seen each other completely. Unashamed and connected. The post-Fall reality of relationship continues to be isolation and fear. We are now born bearing the scars of our earliest parents' sin, and our relationships mirror the heartache of worship lost in Eden.

Because of this sin, Adam and Eve's hiding in the bushes was a picture of the distrust humanity would carry into the future. This distrust was not without cause. Adam and Eve had become the center of worship, and when all of humankind is clamoring to be the center, what follows will be the strong taking advantage of the weak. Worship after Eden moved from a beautiful vision of life to a chilling portrait of death.

Enter Cain and Abel, Adam and Eve's two sons. Both attempted to bring a sacrifice to God. The brothers tried to worship outside of Eden. What was once a clear view of God had been clouded by the Fall. Through the story of Cain and Abel, we learn that the problems that have marked the rest of human history have a specific root. All of our broken stories sprout, grow, and flower from corrupt worship. The atrocities of the ages point to the heart of Cain that still beats inside our chests. Murder, jealousy, and autonomy are the postures of worship that Cain modeled for humanity, and the pages of history have reflected his leadership in terrible ways.

Now Abel was a keeper of sheep, and Cain a worker of the ground. In the course of time Cain brought to the LORD an offering of the fruit of the ground, and Abel also brought of the firstborn of his flock and of their fat portions. And the LORD had regard for Abel and his offering, but for Cain and his offering he had no regard. So Cain was very angry, and his face fell. The LORD said to

Cain, "Why are you angry, and why has your face fallen? If you do well, will you not be accepted? And if you do not do well, sin is crouching at the door. Its desire is contrary to you, but you must rule over it." (Genesis 4:2–7)

Why is one brother's worship accepted while the other's is not? The answer is found in God's question to Cain. "If you do well, will you not be accepted?" Notice that God's problem with Cain's offering isn't about the offering itself; it has to do with the person. "If you do well," God says. The problem is with you, not with what you bring.

Often we focus on the format of worship as the most essential element that brings pleasure to God. Sing out of a book or off a screen. Organ or guitars. Green carpet or hardwood. You name it, we can make it something to argue about, as if we believe getting these elements right will somehow make God more pleased with us. What we fail to realize is that these differences are about us, not God. While we argue about suits and ties versus shorts and flip-flops, God looks at our hearts, which is where our worship actually takes root and springs forth in truth or brokenness. David says it like this in Psalm 24:

Who shall ascend the hill of the LORD? And who shall stand in his holy place? He who has clean hands and a pure heart, who does not lift up his soul to what is false and does not swear deceitfully. (Psalm 24:3–4)

In Psalm 51, David again writes, "For you will not delight in sacrifice, or I would give it; you will not be pleased with a burnt offering. The sacrifices of God are a broken spirit; a broken and contrite heart, O God, you will not despise. (Psalm 51:16–17)

True worship is judged in the heart, not external trappings. Today in our churches, two people singing the same songs can find themselves mirroring the story of Cain and Abel. The one who comes in humility and submission will be accepted; the one who comes in selfishness and arrogance will not. Jesus tells a story that reveals this truth and points back to the sons of Adam and Eve.

He also told this parable to some who trusted in themselves that they were righteous, and treated others with contempt: "Two men went up into the temple to pray, one a Pharisee and the other a tax collector. The Pharisee, standing by himself, prayed thus: 'God, I thank you that I am not like other men, extortioners, unjust, adulterers, or even like this tax collector. I fast twice a week; I give tithes of all that I get.' But the tax collector, standing far off, would not even lift up his eyes to heaven, but beat his breast, saying, 'God, be merciful to me, a sinner!' I tell you, this man went down to his house justified, rather than the other. For everyone who exalts himself will be humbled, but the one who humbles himself will be exalted." (Luke 18:9–14)

Just like Cain and Abel, one person's worship is accepted, and the other's is not. It has nothing to do with the location but everything to do with the heart. To exalt oneself in worship is to be rejected; to surrender and fall down in humility is to once again see the face of God. God isn't concerned with the aesthetics of your worship; he looks at the core of who you are. Cain's sacrifice wasn't rejected because of the substance of his offering but because of who Cain was.

The story of Cain reveals what was lost in the Fall. Cain was angry and selfish and demanded that God accept worship on his terms. Just like his parents, Cain wanted to be God, to have God submit to him. Instead of submission and sacrifice, Cain's worship was built on egotism and control. Worship cannot work on these terms.

Many of us bring our worship to God in the same way. We decide what we think is good and acceptable and demand that God bend to our will and agree with us wholeheartedly. The terms of our worship are set by what we love and what we desire. Push back against anyone's personal interpretation of morality and be prepared to get an earful. "The Bible says you can't judge me!" they will shout. Or, "If you really loved me, you would accept me for who I am." These universal ideas show that worship has been altered into something where we are at the center and in control. Like Cain, we demand that God bend his will toward us.

God doesn't accept these terms with Cain, and he won't accept them with us. God wouldn't accommodate Cain's offering, so Cain was left with a choice. He could change or double down on what he thought worship should be. Cain chose the latter.

Cain spoke to Abel his brother. And when they were in the field, Cain rose up against his brother Abel and killed him. (Genesis 4:8)

Instead of listening to the voice of God and changing his heart, Cain decided to rid the world of competing forms of worship. Abel was struck down by the hands of his own family. Cain wouldn't bend his knee in surrender or sacrifice. He became a reflection of his parent's false worship in Eden.

Here in Genesis 4, with the ink of the Garden of Eden story still wet on the pages of history, Cain plunges humanity further into ruin. Not only has humankind rejected the authority and creativity of God, but it has also now rebelled to the point of murder. The worship problem on full display. After the killing, God asks Cain the same question he asked his parents in the Garden, "What have you done?" (Genesis 4:10) The answer to the question is buried beneath the dirt. His brother is dead, as is humanity's worship of God.

In Cain's story, we are faced with a question that relates to our own. As we consider the worship problem in our lives, how will we respond to God's words to Cain? Will we seek to honor God and kill the self, or will we rebel and destroy whatever attempts to diminish our own version of worship? Worship of God is found in surrender and sacrifice. Cain refuses to give either.

In an amazing show of mercy, God didn't kill Cain in retaliation for his actions. Instead, he cursed him, similar to the curses of the Garden, and sent him out in isolation. Cain's worship was rejected, as was Cain himself. However, the echoes of Cain's worship continued far past his own life, even ringing clear in the present.

After the murder of Abel, God gave Adam and Eve another son named Seth. Readers of the story long to see beauty restored through the gift of another child, but humanity had been changed. Humankind would no longer be made in the image of God but born into the rebellion of Adam. His worship has become our worship. His DNA courses through us, rather than the heart of God.

This is the book of the generations of Adam. When God created man, he made him in the likeness of God. Male and female he created them, and he blessed them and named them Man when they were created. When Adam had lived 130 years, he fathered a son in his own likeness, after his image, and named him Seth. (Genesis 5:1–3)

Do you see the shift? In the beginning, we were created in the image of God. After Eden, Adam's children are fathered in his image and likeness. This catastrophic change would result in the world and worship coming apart at the seams. Humanity would now be made in the image of the Fall.

Seth fathered a great nation that reproduced the worship problem in countless numbers of people. As they grew in power and influence, they infused the earth with rejected forms of worship that enticed humanity into further rebellion for the rest of history.

In a story that shows how quickly the worship worship problem permeated the earth, Seth's descendants built a tower in a place called Babel in an attempt to "reach the heavens." (Genesis 11:1–9) They also wanted to be gods, just like Cain. A dominant culture grew and replaced the one true God with impotent gods of their own design. As Seth's family grew worldwide, their forms of worship became the very thing that would compete for the hearts of God's people to come. Like two trains running on separate tracks, the worship of God would run parallel to the false worship established by the children of Adam and Eve.

Chapter 6

Noah and Worship

There may not be a more famous story in the Bible than Noah and his ark full of animals. A giant replica sits in Kentucky—you can buy a ticket and walk through it. The story decorates nursery walls and fills the pages of children's books all over the world. A crazy reality when you consider that the story is really about thousands of people being drowned in a worldwide flood. Not the kind of lullaby to put a kid to sleep.

I love this story as well, but it is more than God saving a good guy from a flood. The story of Noah and the ark has a direct correlation to the worship problem from the beginning. It exists to show us how badly we are broken. How far away from home the Fall has taken us. The worship problem is rooted deep within the human heart, farther than anything we can do to reach it.

Robert Louis Stevenson's famous work, *The Strange Case of Dr. Jekyll and Mr. Hyde*, is a masterpiece of fiction that depicts a man at war with his evil alter ego. The novella highlights the struggle of human nature between good and evil. As the story progresses, Dr.

Jekyll comes to grips with the reality that his evil counterpart, Mr. Hyde, is going to overcome him completely—Jekyll will be lost forever. His murderous and wicked alter ego is too strong to defeat. Upon realizing this reality, Jekyll writes his final confession. The novella ends with the words, "I bring the life of that unhappy Henry Jekyll to an end." The worship problem is a lot like this.

As humanity moves further away from the perfect worship of Eden, the chaos of rebellion grows stronger and louder. What filled the vacuum of lost worship was a world of selfishness and hate, a series of events that led humanity entirely into darkness.

The LORD saw that the wickedness of man was great in the earth, and that every intention of the thoughts of his heart was only evil continually. And the LORD regretted that he had made man on the earth, and it grieved him to his heart. (Genesis 6:5–6)

Notice the state of humanity's heart: Every intention of the thoughts of his heart was only evil all the time. Everything that had been good and perfect was now corrupted and broken. Created in the image of God, humanity had morphed into the opposite. Like a worldwide pandemic, or Dr. Jekyll overtaken by Mr. Hyde, creation was now utterly and completely broken, sick, and lost, along with the worship it had been created to enjoy.

It is not hard to see how our world today parallels the world Noah lived in. The heart of humanity still seems to be "only evil continually." Genocide, abuse, corruption, greed, abortion, and murder dominate the headlines of our day.

Our culture is obsessed with violence, gore, and eroticism. The entertainment industry makes billions of dollars putting things on big and small screens that mimic and glorify the rebellion stemming from the Fall. If those who professed to be worshippers of God didn't engage with this content, the entire industry would be bankrupt in months, and yet they thrive. Our dollars and viewership drive the industry's wealth and success. Movies and bingeable shows fill our DVRs with images of the very things that moved the heart of God to such grief and pain that he told Noah to build a boat. It is into this kind of world that God appeared to Noah, commanding him to build an ark.

Now the earth was corrupt in God's sight, and the earth was filled with violence. And God saw the earth, and behold, it was corrupt, for all flesh had corrupted their way on the earth. And God said to Noah, "I have determined to make an end of all flesh, for the earth is filled with violence through them. Behold, I will destroy them with the earth. Make yourself an ark of gopher wood. Make rooms in the ark, and cover it inside and out with pitch. (Genesis 6:11–14)

Noah did precisely what God asked him to do and watched as animals of all kinds marched two by two into his giant creation. With Noah and his family safely inside the ark, judgment rained down upon the earth for forty days and forty nights. The world God had created was buried beneath a crushing mountain of water, killing the false worship that had made a mockery of his heart.

Why did God choose Noah? The Bible says it was because he was righteous, but don't let that big churchy word scare you or confuse you. Righteous simply means that Noah was the only man in the whole world who was trying to be faithful to God and submit to what he had been created to be. While everyone else had run as far away from God and the Garden as possible, Noah lived in a way that said he still loved God and longed to return.

Noah was a righteous man, blameless in his generation. Noah walked with God. (Genesis 6:9)

Notice the familiar language? Noah walked with God. Again, we see Garden of Eden talk, reminding us of Adam and Eve walking with God in the beginning. Because of Noah's righteousness, God wanted to do something remarkable with him. He was going to start over and attempt to re-create a broken world with the most faithful man on the planet.

The scene of Genesis 7 is a familiar one. Just as in the beginning, the earth is covered by water—lifeless. Everything that had stood as shining examples of God's perfect creation was now buried beneath the crushing weight of water. Eden was lost. Not only would humankind no longer have access to the sanctuary of God, the sanctuary no longer existed. Beneath the wet face of the ocean's depths lay the entirety of humanity. Families wiped out, along with the cities and towns that housed them.

For some, the story of the flood gives ammunition to the idea that the God of the Old Testament is cruel and vindictive, set on death and retribution. But God's heart isn't driven by hatred—it beats with love. God isn't willing to let humankind run so far into the darkness that they won't be able to return to the light. He isn't willing to allow the evil of Mr. Hyde to win the day. God's judgment is toward the sin that has corrupted his people. Beneath the inky blackness of the deep lies a chance for a new beginning. A hope of worship restored.

Floating on top of a world that was lifeless once again, there rested a single vessel filled to the rafters with a remnant of life. Inside its walls, encased in a rudderless cocoon of wood and pitch, floated the preservation of life. Creation would survive—God had made provision for its survival. Noah, the righteous, would take the created world and bring it to safety. Noah, the righteous, would provide a new beginning for humankind. Amid death and destruction shone a glimmer of hope.

The waters eventually subsided. Noah and his family entered a new era. Nothing remained of the world they had known. Stepping out of the ark, blinking in the sunlight, was like stepping onto another planet. The earth had changed. It was time to start again.

Noah's first act after leaving the ark shows why God had chosen him for salvation. Noah loved God and longed to connect with him through restored worship. He built an altar and made sacrifices, taking a renewed posture of surrender. Could it be that worship had been returned to what it was before?

God spoke to Noah as he had spoken to Adam in Eden. He made him the same promises, gave the same commands. "Be fruitful and multiply," God said. "Rule over my creation." (Genesis 9:1–2) Noah, in place of Adam, inherited a world free of the corruption that had gripped it.

As we read with bated breath, we wonder, will it work? Can the worship problem be solved by the most righteous person on earth? The sad truth seen in Noah is that even the most faithful person cannot fix the problem of rebellion birthed in the beginning. Sin will continue to be part of the human story, and this time it won't be enticed by the words of a serpent. This time no serpent is needed. Noah, the righteous one, the only faithful person on the earth, will be the one who displays that sin isn't a disease that can be washed away by a flood. It lives inside of us.

The joy of Noah's worship was quickly overshadowed by the grips of the worship problem that still lived within him. He planted a vineyard, symbolic of a new garden, but it wasn't created for worship. Instead of worship fueled by selflessness, he made wine and drank until he passed out. Adam's replacement lay in his tent naked and drunk. The most righteous heart couldn't fix what sin had broken.

God was still faithful. Hope was not lost. God promised, through the sign of the rainbow, that he would never flood the earth again. A flood is unnecessary—every generation now knows that even if every evil person in the world was removed and only the most righteous remained, sin would still rear its horrid head and proclaim its power and dominance over the human heart. The answer to humanity's helplessness and slavery to sin can't be found in trying harder or becoming better. Our Mr. Hyde cannot be put down by human will. The utter darkness that sin has created in the human heart can't be remedied by water. It requires something much stronger.

"Whoever sheds the blood of man, by man shall his blood be shed, for God made man in his own image. (Genesis 9:6)

Once again, creation language is used to orient humanity around the severity of the worship problem. Blood, not water, would be required to bring freedom from the guilt of Adam, Eve, and Cain's perverted worship.

Matthew 27 finds Jesus in the last stages of crucifixion. His body is failing. His breath is slow. For three hours—noon until three in the afternoon—it has been dark. Just as in Genesis 1, darkness covers the face of the earth. However, this time, there won't be a voice commanding the dark to become light. The voice that called the sun into being now speaks with labored breath: "My God, my God, why have you forsaken me?" (Matthew 27:46)

The gathering storm clouds won't wipe the earth clean of humanity by a deluge of water. Instead, blood and water will run down as one, dripping from the toes of him who spoke the light into being. The voice that sang the morning into existence will yell out and surrender himself to the darkness. No ark will save Jesus from the deluge that evil had brought once again. Jesus will bear the consequence of what sin had birthed, alone and without a shield.

But the darkness will not hold him. This time, sin will not rule the day. Like Noah stepping out of the ark into the light of a new day, Jesus walks out of his tomb. But unlike Noah, Jesus will not stumble and fall. He will re-create worship forever. After his resurrection, Mary will mistake him for the gardener, and she will worship. Eden is on the horizon once again. Where Adam, Cain, and Noah had failed, Jesus has triumphed.

The worship problem will find its solution in the faithfulness and righteousness of one man—it just won't be Noah. Noah shows us that our worship problem runs much deeper than something you and I can fix on our own. On our best days, we cannot take ourselves back to what was lost in Eden. Jesus is the way back home. Jesus now stands in place of the tree of life from the Garden. He is our place of submission and sacrifice. He is the answer to the problem.

Chapter 7

The Solution Takes Shape

After the flood, the world once again ran from God and the worship it had been created for. Cain and Seth were dead, but because of a terrible sin committed by Noah's son-in-law Ham, humanity was once again cursed by God. The worship created by Cain was reborn on the newly re-created earth, and the worship problem forged ahead with restored vigor. It is in this new world of sin and brokenness that God's ultimate plan for renewal and restoration begins to take shape. God had made promises, and God always keeps his promises.

In Genesis 12, we meet a man named Abram, living in a land called Haran. Abram is wealthy and prosperous; his landholdings are vast, as are his flocks. Abram is diversified in industry and business, an Old Testament Bill Gates or Steve Jobs. In our day, Abram would be considered a mogul, smiling back at us from the cover of glossy magazines containing articles on success and how to diversify our portfolios. He had a lot to lose if he were to leave it all behind.

Now the LORD said to Abram, "Go from your country and your kindred and your father's house to the land that I will show you. And I will make of you a great nation, and I will bless you and make your name great, so that you will be a blessing. I will bless those who bless you, and him who dishonors you I will curse, and in you all the families of the earth shall be blessed."

So Abram went, as the LORD had told him, and Lot went with him. Abram was seventy-five years old when he departed from Haran. And Abram took Sarai his wife, and Lot his brother's son, and all their possessions that they had gathered, and the people that they had acquired in Haran, and they set out to go to the land of Canaan. (Genesis 12:1–5)

There is much to see in these five short verses. They are action-packed and full of ramifications for the story of worship restoration. The most important thing to notice is that God is the initiator of the relationship. Abram wasn't looking for God. He wasn't spending his days working and scheming on a plan to save the world from its worship problem. He was simply a guy living his life and finding success. Because of his success, Abram—whom God later renamed Abraham—had a lot to lose, which made it even more surprising that he was actually willing to leave it all behind.

So why would he go? What causes someone to leave the things that are dearest to them for the dangers of the unknown? On June 6, 1944, thousands of young men offered themselves as sacrifices on the sandy beaches of Normandy, France. They had willingly left home and family to face the dangers of war and evil. Many never made it home, losing their lives in service to something greater than themselves, lives of surrender and sacrifice poured out in acts of selflessness.

When we are brought face-to-face with something bigger than ourselves, we are faced with a choice. We can surrender to it or push against it in self-preservation. The greatest generation moved toward the horrors of World War II willingly because of devotion to their country. They saw the preservation of freedom as more valuable than their lives.

In the same way, when we see God, we are presented with a choice. Our response to the revelation of God defines the heart of our worship—the choice between him and the self. When God appeared to Abraham, he immediately knew that God was worth giving up everything in obedience. God was bigger than his wealth, family, or security. Our vision of God is what fuels our response of obedience and surrender.

The call of Abraham gives us a clear understanding of God's means to save us. He will be the one to fix our worship problem. His call is our only hope of salvation. As God calls you into a relationship with himself, don't feel pressured to make yourself into something that you're not. The worship problem cannot be fixed by your effort. God will be the one who does the hard work, to alter who we are into what we are meant to become. His simple call will be to leave and follow. Like Abraham, our first move back toward a relationship of worship is surrender.

The difficulty is that surrender flies in the face of how we are wired. From birth, we are taught to believe that our ideas are the most important and that real power is getting people to obey us. Great tension lies in the fact that our relationship with God cannot exist on these terms. We aren't in a position to call God into our plans and demand that he bless them. God will remedy our worship problem by calling us away from what we are building back toward his kingdom.

Think of Jesus and his disciples. He rolled up to a group of fishermen and invited them to drop their nets and follow him without even telling them where he was going. Since childhood, the only thing these men had ever known was fishing. To follow Jesus would mean much more than simply leaving a job—it would require leaving security, their entire identity. They were fishermen, not trained rabbis or educated men, and yet Jesus looked at them and said, "Follow me." Just like Abraham, the move toward restoration was a move away from self and toward the call of God. Jesus says to those who want to follow him:

"If anyone would come after me, let him deny himself and take up his cross daily and follow me. For whoever would save his life will lose it, but whoever loses his life for my sake will save it. For what does it profit a man if he gains the whole world and loses or forfeits himself? (Luke 9:23–25)

Jesus will ask you to leave what you have built and controlled so that you can have him instead. He desires to replace your need to manage your life with the surrender that comes through worship. It looks different for different people, but the result is the same—lives remade into the image of Jesus.

In the Bible, Jesus never called two people the same way. His call was always fashioned uniquely around the person being called. To fishermen, he said, "Leave your nets." To a wealthy Pharisee, who was convinced his birth made him important and special, Jesus said, "You must be born again." To a rich young ruler whose identity was made up of money and power, Jesus implored, "Sell everything you have, give it to the poor, and come follow me." Jesus was saying to these people, "Leave who you are, what you think makes you valuable, what gives your life meaning, and come follow me. Turn from where you are heading. Come where I am going."

Surrender. Sacrifice. The core of worship. Those who heeded the call of Jesus to leave and follow found their lives and worship renewed and restored. By surrendering what they had and who they thought they were, they gained what was lost and rediscovered who they were created to be. Are we seeking to do the same?

I recently met a guy named Will, who had just moved back to Knoxville from California. He had been working at an excellent job and living in a fantastic community. A few weeks prior, out of the blue, he heard the Holy Spirit say, "You need to quit your job and move back to Knoxville." God said nothing more than that. Will said it was weird and scary but undeniably the voice of God asking him to submit and obey. He did it. He obeyed.

After returning home, his grandmother, who had raised him, became ill and was placed in hospice. His aunt, who was her caretaker, had a mental break leading to hospitalization. In the middle of a family crisis, Will was speaking the words of Jesus. Of course, Will had no idea all that was going to happen when God told him to leave and move back to Tennessee. Through surrender, Will is now seeing the power of God at work through his life of worship. He would have missed the whole thing if he hadn't submitted to Jesus. This is worship. In a small way, it's what Abraham was asked to do.

God's command for Abraham was not without promise. God didn't ask Abraham to leave with nothing to hope for on the horizon. In exchange for his obedience, God made two promises that have shaped the rest of history, promises that would create new hope and bring humanity back toward true worship. Just as God spoke into darkness bringing light, his promises to Abraham work the same way, resonating in our churches and worship to this day. They are the bedrock of God's solution to the worship problem.

The first promise was that God would make Abraham into a great nation. "Wait," you might say, "I thought you just said that the call of God was not about us or our plans." I get how it might be a little confusing. Here is the principle to understand: The call of God is about what he wants to do through us to further his kingdom. If he wants to make you into a great nation, so be it. If he calls you to lose your life through persecution, the way to joy is to follow the call. God made promises to Abraham based on what he planned to do to bless the world. Abraham's job was to submit and believe.

God said that Abraham's descendants would scatter and spread throughout the entire earth. He takes him outside on a starry night and tells him to look toward the sky for an object lesson on how vast these promises would be. One of my favorite things in the world is to lie on a blanket on a clear night looking up. A place in the national park close to my house is so dark people drive from all over to set up cameras and photograph the stars. I have lain in fields there many times, overwhelmed by the power of God in creation. The stars make us feel small and instill wonder as we lie silently taking them in. I like to think of Abraham, on a blanket looking up, listening intently to the voice of God as he lavishes promises upon him.

And he brought him outside and said, "Look toward heaven, and number the stars, if you are able to number them." Then he said to him, "So shall your offspring be." And he believed the LORD, and he counted it to him as righteousness. (Genesis 15:5–6)

Abraham's belief in God was critical. God spoke; Abraham believed, resulting in action. Worship isn't found in saying the right things about God—it is birthed as we hear God speak, and we move at his commands. Abraham's life was a picture of this kind of obedience.

The second promise made to Abraham is even more significant than the first. God says that not only will he bless Abraham with an amazingly large family, but that through this family, the whole earth will be blessed. From the great nation Abraham would father was coming one who would awaken a world that had forgotten who they were. Through Abraham's family, the worship problem was going to be rectified once and for all.

Jesus shines in the darkness as the fulfillment of the second promise, and the church is the living, breathing fulfillment of the first. Abraham had no way of knowing how God was going to come through on any of it. Still, God gave Abraham a front-row seat to how his heart was going to act and bring final restoration to the problem of sin. In his promises to Abraham, God was making his move toward killing the worship problem and delivering his people back into a relationship with him.

When we gather to worship, we often sing songs filled with promises that we make to God, ways that we promise to give him our lives. These are beautiful and appropriate responses of worship; after all, surrender and sacrifice are what worship is built upon. In the midst of all our words of promise stands the beautiful reality that our worship has only been made possible by God himself, who made great sweeping promises and came through on them in the end.

Just like Abraham, God has made promises to us that are the bedrock of our hope and future. Our journey back to Eden won't happen because of our faithfulness to our word; it will come as God is continually faithful to his. As we lift up words of commitment, may they be birthed out of the freedom of knowing they aren't the means of our salvation but the delicious fruit of it. As we are brought face-to-face with the immensity of God, may our obedience flow as naturally as water from a spring. But may it also come as a response of worship and surrender, not as a means of gaining his favor. We won't see the face of God because our surrender and sacrifice has won his favor. We will see his face because of Jesus's surrender and sacrifice on the cross. His faithfulness has made a way for us to become worshippers once again. As the old song says:[1]

> *Great is Thy faithfulness, O God my Father*
> *There is no shadow of turning with Thee*
> *Thou changest not, Thy compassions, they fail not*
> *As Thou hast been, Thou forever wilt be.*
> *Great is Thy faithfulness!*
> *Great is Thy faithfulness!*
> *Morning by morning new mercies I see*
> *All I have needed Thy hand hath provided*
> *Great is Thy faithfulness, Lord, unto me.*

---

[1] Thomas Chisholm, "Great Is Thy Faithfulness" (Carol Stream: Hope Publishing, 1923).

This revelation is what allows us to sing in adoration the words of another favorite hymn, "I Surrender All." Worship is a reaction to the revelation of God.

Chapter 8

Sacrifice

All the promises made to Abraham came true. Even in his old age, the promises of God sprang to life and grew. The whole world would be blessed as Abraham fathered a great nation. When you were a kid, you may have sung a silly song about Father Abraham having many sons and that you were one of them. If you ever wondered what that was all about, now you know. Abraham's surrender and sacrifice led him to see the promises of God spring to fruition. But submission doesn't always come without pain and hardship.

It won't always be easy to worship through surrender, and even in surrender, the path forward won't be without peril. God doesn't promise ease; he promises to be with us in the fight. Sometimes we will lose sight of his promise and fall into fear. There will be times where we retreat back into the lie of autonomy and seek out false worship once again. Abraham was no different. The good news is that for all the ways we are unfaithful to our promises, God will always be faithful to his. He will always be the one to make and keep the promises that bring restoration to worship, as proven in the continuing story of Abraham and God's covenant with him.

Covenant is a term that permeates the pages of the Bible. To understand how God's promises work, one must be familiar with the concept. When boiled down to its purest form, a covenant was an unbreakable promise between two parties. It was much more than merely giving your word on something.

A modern-day example of a covenant would be signing a contract. Maybe you have taken out a loan or started a job where you signed a formal agreement. In signing these documents, you promise to do something in exchange for something else. You make a promise. Through the covenant in Genesis, God makes an unbreakable promise to Abraham. Modern-day contracts involve pen and paper with the threat of litigation if one party fails to uphold their end of the deal. In Abraham's day, devoid of a modern system of courts and law, different means were used to enter into this unique agreement.

The ancient covenant may seem strange to our modern sensibilities. The two parties instituted the covenant by taking an animal, or animals, and killing them together. When the sacrifice was complete, the dead animals were then halved and laid apart from one another, making a path between the parts. Those making the covenant then walked together between the bloody parts of the sacrificed animal, completing the agreement. This gruesome action created a visible picture that communicated the penalty of failing to live up to the deal. It was a way of saying, "If I break my promise, let what happened to these animals happen to me." Needless to say, entering into a covenant was not to be taken lightly.

In Genesis 15, God made a covenant with Abraham with a striking caveat to the norm. Instead of Abraham and God walking through the animals of the covenant together, God caused Abraham to fall into a deep sleep. While Abraham dreamed, God walked through the symbol of covenant fidelity alone. This simple action is the burning heart of God's plan to fix the worship problem. He was taking the responsibility upon himself alone to see it mended.

God knew that we would be unfaithful to any covenant we made. We are wired from birth to break promises because of the worship problem. The image of Jesus should overcome us as we draw a line from this covenant act with Abraham to the fulfillment of it on the cross. As God walked through the bloody pieces of sacrificed animals while Abraham slept, his mind was already on the image of his son bleeding and dying as a result of our unfaithfulness. We would be the ones to break the agreement. Jesus would be the one to make amends. He would be the one to restore worship; we would be the ones to watch and react to the magnitude of his work. While Abraham dreams, God once again promises him that he will father a great nation that will bless the world and that he will be faithful to bring it to pass.

We always like to think that if God spoke to us directly and made huge promises, we would rejoice and believe with ease. We know from history and from our own hearts that this is not the case. For Abraham, there was one massive problem to the promise God had made. He and his wife were old—way past the age where they could become parents of an infant son. How could the promise of God to be fulfilled through people who were too old to have children? This is where the submission and trust of Abraham takes a turn back toward the dark.

When we attempt to step in and reshape God's promises into something we can control, the result will always be pain. I'm sure you and I could sit and swap stories of how this has played itself out in our lives on multiple occasions. Abraham discovers this truth in a way that results in the world moving once again toward broken worship. Impatient, Abraham's wife, Sarah, takes matters into her own hands and sends her servant Hagar to sleep with Abraham. Since Sarah is too old to have a child, she will help God through a plan of her own.

God never needs our help to fulfill his promises; he only desires surrender and trust. Abraham submits to his wife and fathers a son named Ishmael with Hagar. None of this was God's plan. Their disobedience resulted in conflict and tension that exists to this day as nations following Islam seek to remake the world through false worship. Because of Abraham and Sarah's sin long ago, the worship problem takes on new forms that survive in the present. But God is always faithful.

Even in the face of disobedience, God does not revoke his promises. God does not become unfaithful when we prove ourselves to be. Even in our mistakes, God remembers his promises and remains true to them. This is the hope of the gospel. Whatever mistakes have defined you and moved you away from the heart of God, remember that his heart has never strayed from you. Your hope has never been based on what you have done. It has always been based on what he has promised to do.

Abraham was no different. God forgave Abraham and reiterated his plan to make Abraham a father through his wife, Sarah. God was going to bless the whole world through this promised child. Abraham once again moved into a posture of surrender.

In a miracle birth, Abraham and Sarah are gifted with a son of promise. Remember, as you surrender in worship, God will always come through, even when it seems impossible. When it feels as if the promise is forgotten or long in coming, God has never failed to deliver on his covenant words. Abraham's son, Isaac, is proof of God's commitment to his plan to restore worship and intimacy.

It is also through Isaac that God shows what this restoration will ultimately cost. Worship will not come cheap or easy. It will require sacrifice and submission on the greatest level imaginable. Years later, when Isaac is a young man, God again commands Abraham.

After these things God tested Abraham and said to him, "Abraham!" And he said, "Here I am." He said, "Take your son, your only son Isaac, whom you love, and go to the land of Moriah, and offer him there as a burnt offering on one of the mountains of which I shall tell you." (Genesis 22:1–2)

God asked Abraham to take the thing that meant the most to him in the world and give it away in worship. Once again, just like when he first called Abraham from his home and people, God was asking Abraham to surrender what he loved, but this time the stakes were even higher. Abraham had waited a lifetime for God to deliver on his promises, and now it seemed as if God was taking it away. It must have seemed so unfair. Until this point, he had followed the voice of God without question—how could he continue to do so now? Could Abraham's surrender in worship run this deep?

As a father of four daughters, I cannot imagine this choice. I have often put myself in Abraham's shoes and wondered where my heart would have gone if the decision had been mine. Am I willing to offer my family to God as an act of surrender and obedience? Do I trust his goodness and promise that deeply? Abraham did. His response to God's request sends chills up and down my spine. In the most significant sign of submission yet, Abraham took his son Isaac and headed toward the place of sacrifice.

So Abraham rose early in the morning, saddled his donkey, and took two of his young men with him, and his son Isaac. And he cut the wood for the burnt offering and arose and went to the place of which God had told him. (Genesis 22:3)

He obeyed. He surrendered to the voice of God and saddled his donkey to go and make sacrifices. Abraham was a walking and breathing picture of what it means to worship the living God.

What has God called you to surrender? Where has God asked you to step out with enormous amounts of faith to see his promises on display in your life? Do not hear me wrong. This is the point where TV preachers ask you to give them your money so they can buy a bigger house. We aren't talking about faithless men and get-rich-quick schemes—we are talking about your life. About living in such a way that the things most precious to you are available for the kingdom of God—your family, your school, your job, your home, even your life. This is where true worship begins. It doesn't start or end with a great song on Sunday. You don't have to buy a ticket for the next great worship night that rolls through your city. Worship begins right where you sit with the act of surrender. At times, scary surrender.

What follows is a picture of what the gospel of Jesus will become. Abraham took his son Isaac and began to climb the mountain of Moriah to the place of sacrifice. Isaac asked his father the heart-wrenching question, "Father, where is the lamb for the offering?" Abraham answered with absolute faith, "Son, the Lord will provide." At the top of the mountain, Abraham bound his son and laid him down on the place of sacrifice. He raised the knife in obedient faith to offer what was most precious to him. But the knife would not fall. God would provide. Amid Abraham's stunning obedience, a voice thundered from the heavens.

But the angel of the LORD called to him from heaven and said, "Abraham, Abraham!" And he said, "Here I am." He said, "Do not lay your hand on the boy or do anything to him, for now I know that you fear God, seeing you have not withheld your son, your only son, from me." And Abraham lifted up his eyes and looked, and behold, behind him was a ram, caught in a thicket by his horns. And Abraham went and took the ram and offered it up as a burnt offering instead of his son. So Abraham called the name of that place, "The LORD will provide"; as it is said to this day, "On the mount of the LORD it shall be provided." (Genesis 22:11–14)

God honors the surrender, sacrifice, the worship of Abraham with provision. In his willingness to sacrifice Isaac, God had seen his heart.

God didn't need Isaac's life for worship to be restored. Isaac wasn't even close to being qualified to bring it about. Through Abraham's faith, God paints pictures of his future plan to bring the people he loves back into the fellowship of the Garden. The restoration of true worship would require a perfect lamb. It would take a perfect son. God would have to provide the true sacrifice for everyone.

Just like Abraham was called to take "his only son, whom he loved," as a symbol of sacrifice, God would hear his own beloved son speak similar words to a Pharisee named Nicodemus.

"For God so loved the world, that he gave his only Son, that whoever believes in him should not perish but have eternal life. For God did not send his Son into the world to condemn the world, but in order that the world might be saved through him. (John 3:16–17)

The ram caught in the thicket, in place of Isaac, was the picture of how worship would be renewed. Isaac was not the son who could reverse the worship problem; his life wouldn't have been enough. But God's own son would be. The sacrifice of Jesus and the power of his resurrection would fulfill all the promises God made to Abraham. God had walked through the broken pieces of sacrificial animals, ratifying their covenant, knowing that he would bear the weight to keep it. God won't demand surrender and sacrifice from us to restore worship; he will give it himself.

One of my favorite hymns of all time, "O Sacred Head, Now Wounded,"[2] says it beautifully.

What thou, my Lord, hast suffered
Was all for sinners' gain
Mine, mine was the transgression
But thine the deadly pain
Lo, here I fall, my Savior
'Tis I deserve thy place
Look on me with thy favor
Vouchsafe to me thy grace.

---

[2] Bernard of Clairvaux (1091-1153), "O Sacred Head, Now Wounded," trans. James W. Alexander, 1830.

Chapter 9

Freedom through Surrender

———

The story of Abraham and the promises God made him become the backdrop for the rest of the Bible. They are promises that move the worship problem down the path toward a solution. Abraham fathered Isaac, who fathered Jacob whose name was changed to Israel, who fathered sons who became heads of the twelve tribes that ultimately became the nation of Israel. Whew, did you follow all that? Long story short, God remembered Abraham and came through on his promise to make him into a great nation. Once again, God always does what he says he will do, regardless of our ability to do the same.

However, as Genesis ends and Exodus begins, it seems like the promises of God have hit a snag. Abraham's descendants had found refuge from famine in the land of Egypt and favor in the court of Pharaoh. As Exodus begins, we read about the ascension of a new Pharaoh who is singing a different tune. Because God had blessed Israel, they had multiplied and become a perceived threat to his power. The sheer number of Israel's population intimidated the new

Pharaoh and made him nervous. He feared they would revolt and take over the nation. Pharaoh's solution is to enslave them and use them for forced labor. God's promised people now find themselves in chains.

Slavery has a dark place in American history. It wasn't long ago that white men from Europe loaded African families against their will onto slave ships headed to the United States. While it seems like ages ago, a quick glance at the history books tells us we aren't that far removed from the horrors of slavery in our midst. The consequences of an entire nation's sin still echo today as racial tension dominates the landscape of our communities. We have an up close and personal understanding of the lasting effects slavery has on a nation. The effects of slavery aren't quieted when physical realities change. The same is true of spiritual bondage.

Through slavery, God gives us a picture of the spiritual reality of humanity at the end of Genesis. He uses its horrors to show us what the worship problem really entails. The people of Israel believed their bondage was only physical, but God knew it ran much deeper. The loss of worship in Eden had resulted in much more than just humanity running away to make bad decisions. At its core, it had brought with it a prison that couldn't be escaped without God's intervention. God was going to use Israel's physical reality to highlight the issue that all humanity faces in spiritual slavery. The same is true of us today. In Christ, God is leading people out of spiritual bondage back into true and restored worship. Paul writes in his letter to the Romans:

Do you not know that if you present yourselves to anyone as obedient slaves, you are slaves of the one whom you obey, either of sin, which leads to death, or of obedience, which leads to righteousness? But thanks be to God, that you who were once slaves of sin have become obedient from the heart to the standard of teaching to which you were committed, and, having been set free from sin, have become slaves of righteousness. (Romans 6:16–18)

After life in the Garden, humanity couldn't mend their shattered relationship with God. This is why God allowed his chosen people to fall into slavery in the first place. It was all part of his plan to restore worship. He was preparing them for liberation in a way that would demand they walk in the same kind of obedience as their father, Abraham. Just like God told Abraham to leave and go to a land that was promised, God was going to ask the same of Israel. Asking an entire nation to leave their home is, however, a much larger proposition than the same command to just one person. To ask surrender and sacrifice of millions of people at once would take a work of God. The story told in Exodus cannot be described any other way.

Had Israel stayed prosperous in Egypt, they wouldn't have been excited to leave their wealth behind to follow the voice of God into the wilderness. But God, in his perfect plan, placed Israel in a situation where they would beg to leave for the unknown. An enslaved nation would jump at the chance for freedom and head to a land filled with promise. Through slavery, God provided his chosen people with a means to understand what they really needed to be free. It was through the reality of slavery that God loved his people toward worship restoration. God does the same thing for us.

If you are walking through a time that feels like prison or slavery, know this about God: He loves you. His heart beats with kindness toward you. Your prison isn't a sign that God has turned his back on you—it's the very means he wants to use to call you into freedom and worship. We aren't usually willing to take giant leaps of faith out of security and comfort. It is in times where the ground seems to be moving under our feet that we look to heaven and ask God to move. Or as the writer of Hebrews puts it:

Consider him who endured from sinners such hostility against himself, so that you may not grow weary or fainthearted. In your struggle against sin you have not yet resisted to the point of shedding your blood. And have you forgotten the exhortation that addresses you as sons?

"My son, do not regard lightly the discipline of the Lord,
nor be weary when reproved by him.
For the Lord disciplines the one he loves,
and chastises every son whom he receives."

It is for discipline that you have to endure. God is treating you as sons. For what son is there whom his father does not discipline? (Hebrews 12:3–7)

The discipline of God isn't a sign of his anger but of his love and kindness. The very thing that feels like his frown is what moves you toward the place where you can see his smile. God places us in circumstances that force us to turn from what has put us in chains so that we can see how he will work in power to bring us freedom. In these places, the work of redemption shines the brightest. Israel learned this lesson in a powerful way. God intended to free his people from slavery so they might worship once again. This is the point of the story. God wants a people he can walk with in worship. It is what he desires from us as well.

The story of Israel's rescue from slavery into freedom becomes the setting for us to understand the work of Jesus on the cross. It isn't an overstatement to say that if a person lacks a basic grasp of the events leading to the exodus from Egypt, they will miss the weight of what Jesus says and does in the days leading up to his execution. In many ways, the steps Jesus walks toward the cross retell Israel's story. Jesus acts out Israel's slavery and God's means of bringing them freedom, ultimately leading to the cross. Through Israel's story, we get a front-row seat as God spells out what restored worship is going to cost.

During those many days the king of Egypt died, and the people of Israel groaned because of their slavery and cried out for help. Their cry for rescue from slavery came up to God. And God heard their groaning, and God remembered his covenant with Abraham, with Isaac, and with Jacob. God saw the people of Israel—and God knew. (Exodus 2:23–25)

God hears his people groaning and decides to act. Notice why he is working—because of the promise he made to Abraham. Remember, our only hope in having our worship problem remedied lies in God's faithfulness to his promises. Even amid Egyptian slavery, God remembers the day he made the covenant promises to Abraham alone. We will only be saved as God remembers and acts on our behalf. He alone holds the keys to freedom and life.

What are you enslaved to? Why have you been crying out in pain, wondering if there is anyone who hears or sees? You weren't made for slavery. You were made for freedom. You were made to experience God through intimacy and worship. However, freedom and right worship will only come through surrender and sacrifice. Are you willing to relinquish the need to be God—or as the serpent said in the beginning, "to become like God"—to be re-created into who you were always meant to be?

For many, the answer is no. Church services are filled with people who have found themselves in the grips of modern-day slavery to sin. We sing songs of freedom but live in ways that plunge us deeper into bondage. Jesus stands calling out for us to let him lead us out of captivity and into the freedom of worship, yet we remain chained. Many believe that their chains are actually the signs of their liberty. That the power to dictate and make decisions are what will bring joy. It is God's kindness that allows the weight of slavery to birth within us a desire for true freedom. God longs for you to surrender to him in worship so that you may find yourself running to freedom.

Surrender. Sacrifice. Worship. Are you ready for freedom? God wants to bring it to you. Jesus won it for you at great cost to himself. As Israel is freed from bondage, we find that the chains that hold us can only be loosed by the faithful power of a promise-keeping God. As Israel waits for deliverance, they are ushered into the promise of God. Through the miraculous, God will reveal his plan to solve the worship problem once and for all.

Chapter 10

Here I Am

God came to Israel's rescue in the unlikeliest of ways. Moses was the last person we would expect God to task with bringing an entire nation out of slavery into freedom. You may think the same thing about yourself. I know I do. Moses was an Israelite who had escaped a nationwide infanticide ordered by Pharaoh. Through extraordinary circumstances, he ended up being raised in the court of Pharaoh himself.

Later in life, Moses murdered an Egyptian guard after seeing him beat a Hebrew slave. He then fled into the wilderness in fear for his life. As he hid in the desert, he became an ordinary shepherd in service to his father-in-law for forty years. I'm sure he expected to live his entire life in the regret and shame of his past, tending sheep in the desert.

I'm a sucker for a good sports movie—they seem to inspire on a level other films can't. One of my favorites is the classic basketball story *Hoosiers* about a disgraced coach who moves to a small town in an attempt to find redemption. My favorite scene is where Coach

Dale asks the town drunk, Wilbur "Shooter" Flatch, to join him as an assistant coach.

Shooter is petrified as he stands on the court in front of people who know his past and aren't afraid to remind him of it. His son, who plays on the team, is also ashamed of his father. The tension is thick. In a stunning move, Coach Dale heads over to the referee during a heated moment and asks to be thrown out of the game. The shocked ref doesn't understand at first but eventually grants Coach Dale's wish. With head hung low in false sorrow, Coach Dale hands the clipboard to Shooter and tells him that he'll have to coach the rest of the game on his own. With shaking hands and voice, sweat pouring down his face and onto the court, Shooter draws up the play that leads the team to victory. An unexpected hero overcomes a past marked with regret.

Moses wasn't expecting to be the means God would use to deliver his people. But despite all his flaws, Moses would be the tool God used to bring freedom and restored worship. God isn't dependent on the previous faithfulness of the person he chooses— he only needs a life marked by surrender in the present. God wants to use us the same way he used Moses—as a tool to bring those enslaved out of slavery and into worship. Your past doesn't matter. Whatever has come before has no bearing on how God wants to use you in the future. Worship is the marker of those God can empower to accomplish the miraculous on his behalf. Moses wouldn't stay a shepherd in the middle of nowhere. He was called to speak to kings to display the glory of the God who had called him.

As we move along through worship history, we see a shift in how some respond to God through worship. In Abraham and Moses, we see a reversal of Cain's rebellion through surrender. Cain had rejected God's call into submission and sacrifice, while Abraham and Moses responded with arms wide open to his will and plans. It is in this posture that the way back to true worship is found.

Have you heard the call of God to relinquish who you want to be so you can become who he wants to transform you into? As we have seen so far, the call of God isn't easy; it doesn't promise comfort and ease. Despite what many false teachers have said, following Jesus doesn't equal money and health. Those who say otherwise will have some explaining to do to the disciples of Jesus who were martyred for their faith.

If you could ask Abraham whether life would have been simpler if he had just stayed home when God called him, I'm sure he would smile and say yes. Still, I'm also sure that if you asked him if his decision to surrender and sacrifice had been worth it in the end, his response would be an even louder YES. If Abraham and Moses had decided against transformation, they would have kept their lives intact but would have missed out on God himself. By holding their lives loosely, they gained a firm grip on God's eternal promises and lived in the realm of the miraculous. The same is true of the disciples of Jesus. Even in death, they gained more than this life could have ever given. Their decision to leave everything and follow Jesus resulted in true life in the end. This is the result of true worship—a life lived to the fullest.

The story of God calling Moses is a famous one. Most of us have probably heard the story of the burning bush at some point in our lives. Moses was a shepherd who spent countless hours by himself tending the flocks of his father-in-law, Jethro. On a day like any other, Moses was drawn to a strange bush that appeared to be on fire but wasn't being consumed by the flames. In curiosity, Moses approached the bush to see what in the world was going on.

The wonder he was about to encounter would only be the start of an amazing life filled with the power of God on display. A voice spoke from the flames and commanded Moses to take off his shoes because the place he was standing was holy ground. God started his relationship with Moses by preparing him to be a worshipper. Holy ground is only found in a sanctuary, a place where God's spirit connects with the earth, a place like the Garden of Eden re-created in the wilderness.

Moses was about to enter into a relationship of worship with God that would change him and bring freedom to a nation that had wandered miles away from the surrender and sacrifice of Eden. Just like Abraham, God was speaking to a man who previously hadn't been looking for him. Out of the bush, God asked of Moses the same things he asked of Abraham. The themes of true worship were the core of Moses's calling: leave and follow. Sacrifice and surrender. God was preparing Moses to lead his enslaved people back into worship once again.

At this point, it would be helpful to point out the collective response of Abraham and Moses to the call of God so we can understand how to orient our lives in the same way. When God calls, we must know how to respond in worship. Both men, and others in the Old Testament, used a specific word to respond to the call of God. When God spoke out of the burning bush and called Moses by name, Moses responded with the Hebrew word, "Hineini." English translations of the Bible translate this word as the phrase, "Here I am," but this beautiful word is so much more than that.

Then Abraham reached out his hand and took the knife to slaughter his son. But the angel of the LORD called to him from heaven and said, "Abraham, Abraham!" And he said, "Here I am." (Genesis 22:10–11)

Moses responded the same way to his call at the burning bush.

When the LORD saw that he turned aside to see, God called to him out of the bush, "Moses, Moses!" And he said, "Here I am." (Exodus 3:4)

Both men gave the same response as God called out their names. Hineini, at its core, is a way of saying, "I see you, you see me, and I am surrendering to what you are going to ask me to do." It would be a mistake to think of "Here I am" as a simple roll call or answering "present," as someone calls your name. What these men are saying is, "I am here and waiting to follow. You have my attention, and I am ready to act."

Others will say the same word as God calls their name later in the Old Testament. Men whom God will also use to march a fallen people back toward restored worship. As these men surrender to the call of God, he uses them for his purpose.

Samuel, the prophet: "Then the LORD called Samuel, and he said, 'Here I am!'" (1 Samuel 3:4)

Isaiah, the prophet: "And I heard the voice of the Lord saying, "Whom shall I send, and who will go for us?" Then I said, "Here I am! Send me." (Isaiah 6:8)

This response allows us to see the movement of God take shape. Many people bemoan the fact that they have been a Christian for decades but have never really seen him move in powerful ways. Is it because he isn't moving, or could the answer be that they have never put themselves in a position to see him move? When God calls us to follow him into the unknown waters of faith, is it possible that our reaction is often to say, "No thanks, that sounds scary, how 'bout we do it a safer way?"

The common response in the Old Testament from those God used to move the needle back toward true worship were those who surrendered to his voice by saying, "Hineini." Here I am. Are we those kinds of people, or are we still living in the broken worship of the beginning where we demanded that God surrender to us? Are we still trying to be God, or are we in a place to hear the call of God and say, "Here I am?"

There may be no better example of this kind of surrender in our modern context than the life of Jim Elliot. Jim was convinced from a young age that God was calling him to leave home and serve the kingdom of God on the mission field. His studies and preparation led him and his wife, Elizabeth, to preach the gospel of Jesus to the Auca Indians in the small country of Ecuador. The danger was overwhelming. The Auca tribe was known for violence and murder —to reach out to them was to place your life in great peril. Jim knew that the call to surrender and sacrifice was not always easy but always led to the heart of God.

Jim's journal entry for October 28, 1949, sums up the heart of worship beautifully as he penned the words, "He is no fool who gives up what he cannot keep to gain what he cannot lose."[3] What a powerful statement of a life devoted to the worship of God. Jim Elliot understood that to gain God, we are required to lay down ourselves. Jesus said it this way:

For whoever would save his life will lose it, but whoever loses his life for my sake will save it. (Luke 9:24)

On January 8, 1956, at the age of 28, Jim and four of his friends were attacked and killed by the Auca Indians on a small beach in

---

[3] Elisabeth Elliot, *Shadow of the Almighty* (New York: Harper & Row, 1958), 144.

the jungles of Ecuador. In his final act of sacrifice and surrender in this life, Jim paved the way for the Auca Indians to know the gospel of Jesus. Soon after his death, his wife and a team of missionaries returned to the Aucas with words of love and forgiveness. They later saw the entire village enter into faith and worship, including those who had taken Jim's life.

A life of sacrifice and surrender will lead to God working wonders through our worship. Moses surrendered to the call of God to go back to Egypt and speak to Pharaoh and order him to let God's enslaved people go. In his obedience, Moses had no idea what extreme power lay on the horizon as God prepared to lead his people into freedom. God desires for us to see the same as we respond to his call with "Hineini."

Moses became God's mouthpiece to the most powerful man on the face of the earth for one reason—that the people God loved could go out from slavery and walk into worship. Moses appeared before Pharaoh and told him this very thing: "Let my people go so that they may go into the wilderness and worship there." The call away from slavery is a call into freedom that culminates in restored worship.

Through Moses's surrender, God would deliver his people out of Egypt with a stunning display of signs and wonders that would end in a ceremony that became the heartbeat of worship for the rest of history. The feast of Passover became the very thing that Jesus himself would use as the picture of what true worship restoration would cost. In this act of deliverance, God gives the most precise picture yet of how worship will be redeemed, restored, and returned to where it was in the beginning.

Chapter 11

Passover

Blood. Frogs. Gnats. Flies. Sickness. Boils. Hail. Locusts. Darkness. These were the signs and wonders brought upon Egypt as time and time again Pharaoh refused to let the people of God go free into the wilderness to make sacrifices and worship.

Pharaoh was a perfect picture of everything worship had become after the Fall. In his unwillingness to yield to God's commands, we see the culmination of Adam and Eve's refusal to surrender in the Garden and Cain's murder of Abel in place of making right sacrifices. In Egyptian worship, Pharaoh was seen as a god, and gods do not bow down to anyone. In his mind and heart, he was the one to whom others surrendered. He was the one to whom the sacrifice was due. Pharaoh would see that God will always reign and rule in the end. Through the last sign brought upon Egypt, God showed powerfully that there was no other being in creation who could rival his claim to true divinity. There was no one else who deserved worship.

In my lifetime, I have probably read C. S. Lewis's *The Chronicles of Narnia* series at least twenty times. I love them. I love the world Lewis created to deliver powerful metaphors of good versus evil and the gospel. In *The Lion, the Witch, and the Wardrobe*, we are introduced to the queen of Narnia, known to Narnians as the White Witch. As the story progresses, the reader learns that the queen is not the rightful queen at all. She has stolen power and placed the entire land under a powerful curse that keeps the citizens enslaved within a perpetual winter.

Her nemesis, however, is the lion Aslan—the most powerful being in Narnia and the creator of the world. Aslan is on a mission to see her removed from power. The struggle between these two forces is a literary triumph as we see the powerful queen wither under the force of Aslan's strength. The White Witch imagines her power greater than the one who spoke the world into existence. She is woefully mistaken, as is Pharaoh in the book of Exodus.

Even as they were enslaved in Egypt, the people of Israel shared Pharaoh's worship problem. In reality, the depth of their slavery ran much deeper, since a rejection of God as the source of worship and surrender always leads to spiritual bondage. But God's heart is always to bring freedom. In Exodus 12, God tells Moses to command the people to ready themselves to leave Egypt, but like God often does, he asks them to do it a peculiar way.

At this point in the story, we would expect God to tell his people to make weapons and prepare for war in an epic *Lord of the Rings*–type showdown against the forces of evil. Instead, God tells his people to prepare a special meal and observe a new holiday as their means of escape. It would be like prisoners being told to ready themselves for freedom by sitting down for Thanksgiving dinner with their families. Why in the middle of a tension-filled night would God want to sit down and have a picnic? The answer is beautiful and holds true for those who know God to this day.

Those enslaved by darkness don't have to pick up weapons to win their freedom. The people of Israel wouldn't be doing the fighting. All they were asked to do was to witness the work of God and then remember forever what he would accomplish on their behalf. Just like Americans remember the first meal of Thanksgiving between the Native Americans and the pilgrims, the people of God would have a meal to remember God's faithfulness and power in leading them from slavery toward freedom. David's beautiful words in Psalm 23 give a perfect picture of this.

Even though I walk through the valley of the shadow of death, I will fear no evil, for you are with me; your rod and your staff, they comfort me. You prepare a table before me in the presence of my enemies. (Psalm 23:4–5)

Often, during the fight, God will ask us to sit and have a meal. It will seem out of place and bizarre when he does it. "God, take this enemy away," we cry. "Please heal this cancer, make this pain stop, bring healing to this relationship, make them stop saying this about me." Sometimes, when the battle is raging the hottest, God will simply call us to sit down and eat. With the sounds of the fight raging all around us, we will rest in the provision of our God. He will remind us that we are his. He will lavish us with the richest of foods. He will be the one to overcome the enemies of life. We are asked to sit and eat and remember. We are asked to worship.

The center of the Passover meal was a lamb without spot or blemish that was to be killed and bled. The blood from the lamb was taken outside and spread over the doorpost of every house. When the angel of death came, he passed over the house that bore the sign of blood. God gave the people a way to make provision for their households, a way to be spared from the coming plague. Worship through surrender and sacrifice was taking on a new and more explicit form. The people were given a picture through sight, taste, and sound of what freedom really cost. They were the ones who deserved to bleed and die because of the rebellion in their hearts, but the blood of a lamb offered them a way to freedom instead.

The voice of John the Baptist in the New Testament thunders as he points at his cousin Jesus and shouts to the people gathered, "Behold, the Lamb of God, who takes away the sin of the world!" (John 1:29) We see the same language in the book of Revelation: "And between the throne and the four living creatures and among the elders I saw a Lamb standing, as though it had been slain." (Revelation 5:6)

The Passover lamb points to God in the form of Jesus as he becomes the one to ultimately bring true freedom and restore the heart of worship to an enslaved people. That is what the lamb of God ultimately does—he brings us back to worship. However, the blood of the lamb of God wouldn't be spread on the wooden beam of a doorpost. It would be spread upon the wooden crossbeam of a Roman execution device as God himself would provide the way out of slavery and back to worship once again. Jesus would re-create Passover as he hung and bled amid the sights and sounds of rebellion.

The people of Israel listened to Moses and did what God had asked them to do. They killed the lambs. They prepared the meal and ate. They took the blood and spread it on the doorposts of their houses. They readied themselves and waited for God to move. He had prepared a table before them in the presence of their enemies. Freedom was coming.

In the middle of the night, the air was filled with the haunting wails of those who hadn't surrendered to God's command to make sacrifice. By refusing to kneel in worship, just like in the beginning, death had come once again. But not to everyone. Those who had blood on their doorposts had been spared. God had provided a means of escape. This time the narrative was changing. God was taking action to reverse slavery and bring about a return to worship.

Pharaoh's unwillingness to bow to the one true God resulted in disastrous consequences for him and his nation. His house wasn't spared. His son was found dead in the middle of a dark night. Years later, Jesus himself would become the firstborn son that succumbed to death because of sin and the curse. God's pain would quake the ground as his beloved son breathed his last. But unlike Pharaoh's son, Jesus wouldn't remain in the grave. His death would defeat the curse and restore lost worship to humanity once and for all.

Pharaoh called Moses in the middle of that dark night and commanded him to take the people of God and go. He would longer set himself against this God who had refused to bow to him. He was defeated, and to continue any longer would result in more heartache and loss. This God was not to be trifled with and was not to be mocked and rejected.

For generations to come, the people of God celebrated Passover to remember God's faithfulness and provision. In fact, this meal is still a significant centerpiece of worship in the modern church. On the night Judas betrayed Jesus in the garden of Gethsemane, Jesus led his disciples through the Passover meal in an upper room. As they ate together, they likely talked about Israel's slavery in Egypt. They would have remembered the stories of the lamb and the angel passing over the houses that had surrendered to the command of God. But on that night, during the sacred meal, Jesus changed everything. He rewrote the script for the rest of history when the Passover meal was observed.

Looking his friends in the eyes, Jesus took the unleavened bread —a central part of the feast—and broke it in front of them. He said, "This is my body of the new covenant. Every time you eat this bread from here forward you are to remember me." The disciples must have been confused. What was Jesus saying? Why remember him instead of Israel's freedom from slavery? Jesus then took a cup filled with wine and said, "This wine signifies my blood; it is a sign of a new covenant given for you; every time you drink this cup, remember me." Even more confusion for the disciples. The blood of Jesus? What was he saying?

Jesus was taking upon himself the responsibility of atonement (an important word we will look at later) for the sins of the world through his blood. The darkness and rebellion that had enslaved creation would now turn its eyes toward God himself as he hung on a cross. After his resurrection, the disciples would understand that everything in Israel's history had been leading up to Jesus. Jesus was the Passover lamb. Jesus was the answer to the promises made to Abraham. Through Jesus, they would find freedom from slavery and enter into true worship.

As the church, we are now invited to remember Jesus through this meal as well. As we take communion together, we are invited to look back to a time when Jesus saw that his people were in slavery to sin and was moved to take action on their behalf. As we remember his act of sacrifice and surrender, we are invited to do the same as our hearts are moved toward worship. God has passed over our sins because of his spotless lamb, Jesus Christ. May this act of love fuel our response in worship.

Chapter 12

Worship in the Wilderness

———————

Countless movies have been made chronicling the journey of the people of God as they left Egypt and walked in the wilderness. From Charlton Heston parting the Red Sea in Technicolor to DreamWorks's animated *The Prince of Egypt,* even Hollywood loves the story of Israel's freedom from slavery and their subsequent wanderings.

What we really find as we look at Israel in the wilderness is more evidence of the worship problem. One would think after being rescued from Pharaoh's grips Israel would want nothing else but to worship the God who had brought them into freedom. But even in their freedom Israel still lives in chains. As they leave the Egyptian oppression, they take with them the memory and the curse of the Garden and worship lost.

After observing the Passover meal, Israel is freed from slavery. No sooner does Pharaoh send them away than he changes his mind and wants them to return. He had just lost his workforce—the labor he had used for years to build his massive kingdom. Pharaoh immediately sends his army to bring them back.

This is the part of the story that makes movie history over and over again. The image of Israel standing before the Red Sea with the army of Egypt closing in behind them invokes all the fear and terror of being trapped with no way out. At this moment, once again God provides miraculously. Moses plunges his staff into the water, and the people of God walk through two walls of water on dry ground. They are saved. They are baptized. God is faithful. Unfortunately, Israel will not be faithful in return.

In Noah, God showed us that even the most righteous man in the world couldn't fix the worship problem embedded deep in the human heart. In the same way, God shows us through the nation of Israel that no matter how many miracles, how many wonders, how much provision he lavished on them, it wouldn't be enough to turn their hearts away from themselves back toward him in worship. The story of Israel in the wilderness, alongside the story of Israel throughout the rest of the Old Testament, reveals that they could never be faithful to God. However, God is always faithful to them.

Many have asked, "How could these people be so stubborn? How could they be so blind?" An honest look into our own hearts will answer the question. How many times has God proved himself faithful in one moment of our lives, and in the very next heartbeat, we have shown our unfaithfulness to him? The critical element of restored worship will rest on the promise of God's faithfulness—it will never hinge on ours.

Two stories stand out to me as we think of Israel's time in the wilderness and how that time reveals how broken their worship would remain. The stories are about God's invitation to come and worship and Israel's rejection of this invitation through a calf made of gold. They both happen at a mountain called Sinai. It is here that God formally introduces himself to his newly freed people. And it is here that they run away from the fellowship God had brought them out of slavery to enjoy. This truth will rise to the surface: God brought them out of slavery, but the bondage of Egypt remained in their hearts. Their bodies were free, but their affection and worship were not.

At my church, we have a ministry for those who battle addiction. If we're honest, we all have addictions of some form in our lives. We desperately seek to medicate hurt, pain, loss, and fear in ways that will dull the ache that such things bring. Not all of us seek relief at the end of a needle or the bottom of a bottle. Some of us do it by working all hours of the day. Or in the soft flicker of a computer screen. The incredible thing about addiction is the power it has over the mind and beliefs of the person addicted. After some time, they begin to identify with their addiction—it becomes their defining trait. They are no longer a daughter or a son—they are an addict. Even after rehabilitation, therapy, and the love of a community, sometimes they still run back to the addiction that promised comfort but always delivers more pain.

At their core, our addictions are symptoms of our worship problem. We save our sacrifice and surrender for the small gods that promise peace but deliver chains. We are afraid to enter into the presence of a holy God because of what he might say or do. Surely all is lost because of who we are? Israel felt and acted the same way in the wilderness. They had been saved from so much. But they still wanted to run back to slavery instead of bowing in worship to God. They will say as much over and over again. "It would have been better if we had never left Egypt," they cry out to Moses. The reality is that Egypt had never left them at all.

In Exodus 19, God introduces himself to the people of Israel. He gives Moses a specific message for them.

While Moses went up to God. The LORD called to him out of the mountain, saying, "Thus you shall say to the house of Jacob, and tell the people of Israel: 'You yourselves have seen what I did to the Egyptians, and how I bore you on eagles' wings and brought you to myself. Now therefore, if you will indeed obey my voice and keep my covenant, you shall be my treasured possession among all peoples, for all the earth is mine; and you shall be to me a kingdom of priests and a holy nation.' These are the words that you shall speak to the people of Israel." (Exodus 19:3–6)

Do you see what God is doing here? He is inviting them back into a worship relationship. He reminds them of everything he has done, all the ways he has been faithful to his promises. He has delivered them out of slavery "on eagles' wings." He follows it up with the charge to remember who they are and to be faithful to him in return. If they will, the relationship from the beginning will be restored. They will become a nation of priests, and the work of Adam as a priest in the Garden of Eden will be renewed. Work and worship will be restored. All it requires is surrender once again. This small passage reveals that God's heart throughout history has been to redeem people out of slavery and place them back into a worship relationship with himself. In Israel's case, he is literally moving nations and nature itself to make it become a reality. For a moment, it seemed like Israel was all in.

All the people answered together and said, "All that the LORD has spoken we will do." And Moses reported the words of the people to the LORD. (Exodus 19:8)

There you have it. The end of the story, right? Happy endings all around. The worship problem is solved. If only. In the very next chapter, the people show their true colors when they decide that God is too scary and they don't want anything to do with him. God has invited them into a relationship, but they don't want it.

Now when all the people saw the thunder and the flashes of lightning and the sound of the trumpet and the mountain smoking, the people were afraid and trembled, and they stood far off and said to Moses, "You speak to us, and we will listen; but do not let God speak to us, lest we die." Moses said to the people, "Do not fear, for God has come to test you, that the fear of him may be before you, that you may not sin." The people stood far off, while Moses drew near to the thick darkness where God was. (Exodus 20:18–21)

Translation: "Moses, God is too scary for us. You go up there and talk to him and then come back and tell us what he said. We will stand waaaaaay over here while you go and meet with him." What a tragedy. What a heartbreaking story from God's perspective. He has done nothing but show the people of Israel love and faithfulness, and now they don't even want to speak with him, much less worship him.

We are guilty of the same. How many times have we stood back from the mountain and tasked others to go up and then tell us what God said? Every year church folks spend buckets of money on conferences and concerts where the "professional" Christians tell us what God has said from the mountain. I'm not against these things. As a matter of fact, I have led worship at these types of events for more than twenty-five years. However, they cannot be the central means of our experience of God. We cannot live our spiritual lives paying money to eat crumbs off other people's tables in an attempt to fill our spiritual hunger with something other than personal interaction with God himself.

Why do we do this? I believe there are many reasons, but at the core, I think many of us are scared, just like Israel, of what we might find on the mountain. When the people of Israel tell Moses they don't want to draw near to God, it's just after he has given them the Ten Commandments. If you have been around Christianity for ten seconds, you have probably heard of these ten rules given by God. They become the bedrock for the complete list of rules God gives Moses on the mountain. As a refresher here they are:

"You shall not take the name of the LORD your God in vain, for the LORD will not hold him guiltless who takes his name in vain.

"Remember the Sabbath day, to keep it holy. Six days you shall labor, and do all your work, but the seventh day is a Sabbath to the LORD your God. On it you shall not do any work, you, or your son, or your daughter, your male servant, or your female servant, or your livestock, or the sojourner who is within your gates. For in six days the LORD made heaven and earth, the sea, and all that is in them, and rested on the seventh day. Therefore the LORD blessed the Sabbath day and made it holy.

"Honor your father and your mother, that your days may be long in the land that the LORD your God is giving you.

"You shall not murder.

"You shall not commit adultery.

"You shall not steal.

"You shall not bear false witness against your neighbor.

"You shall not covet your neighbor's house; you shall not covet your neighbor's wife, or his male servant, or his female servant, or his ox, or his donkey, or anything that is your neighbor's." (Exodus 20:7–17)

When Israel sees this list, they are immediately aware that God has just listed all of the things that they are. They are thieves, they are liars, they are jealous of what other people have, they are adulterers—they are the whole list over and over again. And now, the God who gave the list—the one causing the mountain to smoke and the ground to shake with thunder and lightning—wants to know them intimately through worship. They are afraid of who God is because they are aware of who they are.

We join them in their fear sometimes. I recently sat at coffee with a guy who couldn't believe God could love him. It didn't matter what I said, he couldn't believe God would want anything to do with him. Why? Because of who he was, because of what he had done. He knew himself, and he was aware of how holy God was, and because of that, he believed God was inaccessible to him. Israel stands at the base of the mountain, not wanting to be in the presence of God. They are content to let Moses go into his presence and then report back what he finds there.

How often do we show up at our churches and expect the spiritual disciplines of our pastors to suffice for our experience of God? We hope that somehow tapping into others' spiritual intimacy during an hour-long service will suffice for our worship for the week. Instead of climbing the mountain daily, hourly even, to taste and see the goodness of God for ourselves, we farm out the job to others and then wonder why God seems so far away. To fix our worship problem, we seek to hire substitute worshippers to instill in us a sense of the divine. Still, just like Israel, another person's experience of God cannot replace the personal wonder of entering into his presence through worship.

Worship isn't expressed by singing a song in a room of thousands a couple of times a year. It's found by surrendering who we are by entering into the presence of God moment by moment to discover who he really is. This type of surrender can be scary at first. But what you find will answer who you were created to be and become the balm that heals all the brokenness you have accumulated over years of looking elsewhere. This is the invitation God gives Israel in worship. Still, they are unwilling to accept, and as we will see, they will follow up their rejection by making a version of God that feels safer and tamer. It is a version of God that looks like the Egypt their hearts never left.

Chapter 13

The Golden Calf

God didn't give the Ten Commandments to simply make Israel feel bad about who they were. The commandments were an invitation to be changed into something else entirely. God's invitation into worship is always an invitation to be changed.

The German pastor Dietrich Bonhoeffer famously said, "When Christ calls a man, he bids him come and die."[4] Worship will change who you are and not just on a surface level. In a very real way, worship will kill you. To be made into the image of Christ in worship is to die to the image of ourselves. Our surrender lets God change us into who we were created to be at the expense of what our rebellion has turned us into. Paul says nothing less than this when he writes to the Galatian church:

I have been crucified with Christ. It is no longer I who live, but Christ who lives in me. And the life I now live in the flesh I live by

---

[4] Dietrich Bonhoeffer, *The Cost of Discipleship* (New York: Simon & Schuster, 1995), 89.

faith in the Son of God, who loved me and gave himself for me. (Galatians 2:20)

This is where the answer to the worship problem finds its shape. God had called Israel away from slavery to live as those who were free. He wanted to make them into something new—a beacon that would shine in a dark world pointing the way home. Israel had other intentions for worship. They wouldn't allow God to alter who they were; instead, they would change the image of God to reflect themselves.

We share the same problem with Israel—the desire to make gods that resemble us. However, a god that looks and sounds like us is no god at all—it's an idol. While God is speaking with Moses on Mount Sinai, the people grow impatient and go to Moses's brother-in-law Aaron to demand that he make gods for them to worship.

When the people saw that Moses delayed to come down from the mountain, the people gathered themselves together to Aaron and said to him, "Up, make us gods who shall go before us. As for this Moses, the man who brought us up out of the land of Egypt, we do not know what has become of him." So Aaron said to them, "Take off the rings of gold that are in the ears of your wives, your sons, and your daughters, and bring them to me." So all the people took off the rings of gold that were in their ears and brought them to Aaron. And he received the gold from their hand and fashioned it with a graving tool and made a golden calf. And they said, "These are your gods, O Israel, who brought you up out of the land of Egypt!" (Exodus 32:1–4)

The same people who moments before had shouted in unison that they would obey the commands of God had now made an idol of gold to worship with sacrifices. The God who had brought them out of slavery had been replaced by an idol made from the people's own jewelry. Just like God had commanded a feast to remind them how he had freed them from slavery, the people instituted a new feast in honor of the golden gods they now credited with their freedom. They were already making cheap imitations of the things of God to put themselves at the center of the worship equation once again.

When Aaron saw this, he built an altar before it. And Aaron made a proclamation and said, "Tomorrow shall be a feast to the LORD." And they rose up early the next day and offered burnt offerings and brought peace offerings. And the people sat down to eat and drink and rose up to play. (Exodus 32:5–6)

Why would they do this? Why would they so quickly abandon the God who had brought them into freedom? The answer is as old as the Garden of Eden. In making the golden calf, Israel accomplished two things. First, they were worshipping in a way that was familiar and comfortable to them. They would have seen this type of worship in Egypt, and the calf provided a means of worship that looked like the place that they had left. Instead of surrendering and worshipping in the way God had ordained, they decided to make a form of worship that suited what they thought worship should be. In a moment, they were again a reflection of Cain's worship from Genesis 4, making sacrifices out of their own desires instead of surrendering to God's.

The second reason they made the golden calf was because this god was one that they could manipulate. After all, it very literally was made by their own hands. As they surrendered and made sacrifices to this "god," they were surrendering and sacrificing to something they had made, something they could control. Instead of being remade into the image of God, they had made a god in their own image. What follows is tragic and beautiful at the same time.

On the mountain, while Israel was worshipping the golden calf down below, God told Moses that he would wipe Israel off the face of the earth and start the promise over again through him. Just like Noah, God offered Moses the chance for a fresh beginning.

Moses's response to this proposition revealed that God had already been at work in his life. He was beginning to feel the transformative power of being in the presence of God through worship. He had already started to resonate with God's heart for his people. Instead of seeking to become great, he echoed the heart of God by interceding on Israel's behalf, in spite of their unfaithfulness. Moses even offers his life in exchange for theirs. While Israel is a picture of rebellion and rejection, Moses, by being in God's presence, has been changed into the reflection of what worship truly is.

So Moses returned to the LORD and said, "Alas, this people has sinned a great sin. They have made for themselves gods of gold. But now, if you will forgive their sin—but if not, please blot me out of your book that you have written." (Exodus 32:31–32)

Moses has become the priest God had desired his entire people to become. He offers his life in place of the people. He has heard the voice of the Lord and has become an intercessor; his desire is to point them back to God. He has responded to God's invitation to come up the mountain to worship and has been changed into something different. Moses has been transformed.

Of course, Moses isn't qualified to die on behalf of his people, and God rejects his offer to do so. But Moses isn't off track in making the suggestion. In fact, what Moses suggests is the exact thing that God had in his heart since the curse of Genesis 3. There was a promised one who would come and stand in the place of sinful humanity, but it wouldn't be Moses. One was coming who would hang on a cross and change worship forever. Just as God was rejected at Sinai, Jesus was rejected in Jerusalem. The people of Israel would ask that a murderer named Barabbas be set free in exchange for the death of Jesus himself. When Pilate, the Roman governor of Jerusalem, cried out in surprise, "You would have me crucify your king?" the people responded by shouting, "We have no king but Caesar. Crucify him!" God once again replaced with calves of gold. God replaced with a murderer.

God would remain faithful to his promises. Worship would be restored. The invitation to come and worship will always be extended to those who will hear the call. Just like Moses, those who come into the presence of God will be transformed.

Instead of transformation, I am afraid that in our modern context, we are dangerously close to—and in some instances, already dancing around—calves of gold. For many, worship is no longer an invitation to come and be changed; it is a gathering of those who wish to remain the same. It is filled with people who equate the gospel with words of affirmation and acceptance of their sinfulness instead of their means of escape. Worship has become the shouts and emotions of those who have decided what holiness should look like. Those inviting God into the midst of their own creation.

Worship doesn't exist so that God can make us feel better about our brokenness. God doesn't seek to give us comfort in spite of our imperfections. The love of God we sing about over and over again is not a love that simply accepts who we are or who we desire to be. We have changed love into an affirmation of personal choice. Sexuality and morality now depend on how the individual feels, not on what God has demanded. Now, even for some in the church, to love is to let a person remain as they are. With arms wide open.

God doesn't accept our sin because of his love; his love is the force that seeks to crush it. Worship reveals sin by inviting the worshipper to behold the perfection of God. The grace extended by that invitation is our means of escape and victory over it. Our hope lies in our deliverance, not in our desire to remain the same. We must be changed.

I love Luke 24. On the road to Emmaus, Jesus reveals that he is the fulfillment of all that was spoken of through Moses and the prophets. Just as Moses had led the people to the mountain, through Jesus, God was again inviting a people to the mountain to worship. This time not just to the edge but all the way to the top, giving them full access to his life-altering glory.

Hebrews 12 says it beautifully, speaking of Israel in the wilderness and you and me in the present.

For you have not come to what may be touched, a blazing fire and darkness and gloom and a tempest and the sound of a trumpet and a voice whose words made the hearers beg that no further messages be spoken to them. For they could not endure the order that was given, "If even a beast touches the mountain, it shall be stoned." Indeed, so terrifying was the sight that Moses said, "I tremble with fear." But you have come to Mount Zion and to the city of the living God, the heavenly Jerusalem, and to innumerable angels in festal gathering, and to the assembly of the firstborn who are enrolled in heaven, and to God, the judge of all, and to the spirits of the righteous made perfect, and to Jesus, the mediator of a new covenant, and to the sprinkled blood that speaks a better word than the blood of Abel.

See that you do not refuse him who is speaking. For if they did not escape when they refused him who warned them on earth, much less will we escape if we reject him who warns from heaven. At that time his voice shook the earth, but now he has promised, "Yet once more I will shake not only the earth but also the heavens." This phrase, "Yet once more," indicates the removal of things that are shaken—that is, things that have been made—in order that the things that cannot be shaken may remain. Therefore let us be grateful for receiving a kingdom that cannot be shaken, and thus let us offer to God ACCEPTABLE WORSHIP, with reverence and awe, for our God is a consuming fire. (Hebrews 12:18–29, *emphasis mine*)

Are we offering acceptable worship? We are invited into his presence to be changed into a people set apart in holiness. To proclaim his excellencies as a kingdom of priests. The purpose of the invitation has never changed. The means of the invitation— Jesus making a way for us to come with boldness before God—has been gloriously altered.

The cross of Jesus didn't give God an excuse to sweep our sin under the rug. God cannot merely look the other way from sin—it must be dealt with, and we must be changed. We must sacrifice who we desire to be on the altar of worship, as Paul writes in Romans 12.

I appeal to you therefore, brothers, by the mercies of God, to present your bodies as a living sacrifice, holy and acceptable to God, which is your spiritual worship. Do not be conformed to this world, but be transformed by the renewal of your mind, that by testing you may discern what is the will of God, what is good and acceptable and perfect. (Romans 12:1–2)

And so there it is. Worship will kill you. It is self-sacrifice. It is surrender.

For if we go on sinning deliberately after receiving the knowledge of the truth, there no longer remains a sacrifice for sins, but a fearful expectation of judgment, and a fury of fire that will consume the adversaries. Anyone who has set aside the law of Moses dies without mercy on the evidence of two or three witnesses. How much worse punishment, do you think, will be deserved by the one who has trampled underfoot the Son of God, and has profaned the blood of the covenant by which he was sanctified, and has outraged the Spirit of grace? For we know him who said, "Vengeance is mine; I will repay." And again, "The Lord will judge his people." It is a fearful thing to fall into the hands of the living God. (Hebrews 10:26–31)

May we worship in holiness. May we worship in truth. May the love of God and the grace of God bring us to the knowledge of God. May we accept his invitation to come and worship and be forever changed into his image.

Israel would feel the sting of rejecting this invitation. The calf would be destroyed, as would those who created it. But God in his mercy would still invite his people into worship. Through Moses, God would give the people of Israel a list of rules and regulations that would focus and center worship around the things that would move them back toward holiness. The law would serve as a signpost for this newly freed nation, pointing them toward the heart of the one who had won their freedom.

Chapter 14

The Law and Worship

There may not be a more misunderstood section of the Bible than Exodus, Leviticus, Numbers, and Deuteronomy. For many, the books that contain the law given to Moses on Sinai have become the flyover states of the entire Bible. Regulations about everything from mold to blood leave some readers scratching their heads as to how this could have anything to do with the worship of a holy God. For others, the law is the place to point and scream at the injustices of the wrathful God of the Old Testament. The law is used against the one who spoke it as a reason to not kneel in worship to him.

So how does the law help us understand the worship problem? And how can it serve as a guidebook, giving us the way to fix it? I think the answer is found in two ways. First, the law gives us a clear picture of what God is like. What does God love? What does he hate? How would he live if he were a man, and how would he carry himself in the community of his chosen people were he to walk among them? What is required of those who long to be made holy and set apart once again? Fit for worship in a re-created place where heaven and earth come together as one? The law is God's way of answering these questions for Israel and for us.

Second, the law gives us a clear picture of what we are like. By seeing how God would live if he were an Israelite, we are given a vision of Israel in stark contrast. The nation of Israel didn't resemble God at all. For Israel, the law was like a mirror held up to someone who had never seen what they looked like, and what they saw looking back was broken, dirty, and disheveled. The law gave Israel a picture of how the road back to right worship would be one in which they would be altered and changed.

Have you ever seen a movie or read a story where you couldn't quite figure out who the villain was or what they looked like? God, through the law, pulled the villain of sin out of the shadows and into the light. What had previously lived in darkness now had a giant spotlight shining down on it, removing its mask so the world could see what evil actually looked like. The enemy of worship now had a name and a face. And because of the law, Israel now understood what was required for true worship to be restored.

I am a father of four girls, and I can tell you from experience that kids want boundaries. They want to know what the rules are in advance. Parents who seek to have a good relationship with their children by letting them do whatever they want find that what they thought would bring closeness actually brings contempt. Not only do kids want to know the rules, they also want to know the consequences of breaking them. What happens if I do what you told me not to? Are we talking no electronics for a day or a year? As

Israel's heavenly father, God knew that Israel needed the same kind of love as well.

In Deuteronomy 28—one of the most critical sections of the Old Testament—God commands Moses to tell the people of Israel what will happen if they obey this new law and what will happen if they don't. This section of the Bible is known as the blessings and curses. You should bracket and highlight this section in your Bible. It is crucial to understand how the worship problem will be dealt with.

God gave two separate lists for Israel to hear and understand. The first list was full of blessings that would come from obedience and submission to this new law God had given. Reading the blessings that God promises for obedience should take the reader back to a specific place and time of worship past—the Garden of Eden, where God walked with his creation long ago. It is like seeing the perfection of Eden spring from the mind and mouth of God. As worship is restored, all the things that were cursed begin to find themselves whole once again. Remember Genesis 3, where God cursed humanity, childbirth, the ground, and the serpent? As God lists the blessings for obedience and submission, it reads like an undoing of all the broken things.

"And if you faithfully obey the voice of the LORD your God, being careful to do all his commandments that I command you today, the LORD your God will set you high above all the nations of the earth. And all these blessings shall come upon you and overtake you if you obey the voice of the LORD your God. Blessed shall you be in the city, and blessed shall you be in the field. Blessed shall be the fruit of your womb and the fruit of your ground and the fruit of your cattle, the increase of your herds and the young of your flock. Blessed shall be your basket and your kneading bowl. Blessed shall you be when you come in, and blessed shall you be when you go out. (Deuteronomy 28:1–6)

Do you see the picture of a restored sanctuary? Obedience was the key to Israel's return home and to worship. In addition to these promises, God also said that he would subdue every enemy of his chosen people and lead them into blessing. He would faithfully remember all his promises and bring them to fruition—if they would submit, surrender, and sacrifice in a true return to worship.

The second list God gave stood in stark contrast to the first. It is a list of what would happen if they once again turned away from true worship and chased after other gods. Restating words spoken to Adam in the Garden, God told the people that a refusal to be transformed into who they were created to be would result in the curse being magnified and strengthened. Not only would they find themselves working in futility, but the nation would also be captured and sent into captivity—returned to the slavery God had rescued them from in Egypt.

The choice set before the people was evident. The invitation was amazing. The God who had brought them out of Egypt by his love —leading the way through the Red Sea and the wilderness through awesome displays of power and wonder—was now calling his rescued people into intimacy and worship. Through the law, he was giving them the way to return home, to recover what had been lost in Eden.

The law was given out of the depths of God's love for Israel. Birthed from his desire for her to know him in intimacy once again. Some treat it as if it were a giant buzzkill for anyone who wanted to have a good time. Nothing could be further from the truth. The law wasn't just a long list of things not to do. In addition to things to avoid, the law was also filled with new means of worship and sacrifice that would remove the people's sin and make them fit for renewed worship once again. The only thing Israel was asked to do was obey. Like a child offered a treat if they behave in the supermarket, Israel is now asked to simply honor God, submit to his ways, and seek after him in worship to receive the blessings meant for them from the beginning.

Obedience isn't easy. I'm a walking example of how hard it really is. Because I now have four children, I see it even more clearly. Years ago, my daughter Mae was struggling to not draw on every wall in the house and to not cut up every piece of paper in America. We told her over and over again to stop binge-drawing and cutting. She didn't listen. One fateful night, when my wife was out with friends and I was in charge at home, Mae walked down the stairs and into the living room where I sat. I wish you could see the picture. She had cut off her bangs to the top of her scalp and marked herself head to toe with a permanent marker. She was a walking billboard of disobedience.

The phone call to my wife wasn't fun. "Uh, honey, Mae has done a couple of things to her appearance." On my watch, the worst had come to pass.

We know the end of Israel's story. They wouldn't obey either. Like Adam and Eve, they ignored God's warning and forged a trail in worship that placed themselves at the center of the equation. As a result, Israel ended up conquered by other nations and eventually found themselves in slavery again, crying out for God to hear them and remember his promises, begging to be freed from the oppression they had won through disobedience. Their broken and corrupted worship led them back to ruin and took them back to the loss and heartbreak of the Garden of Eden.

God wasn't surprised by this. He knew that Israel had been made in the image of Adam's corrupted worship. The law was meant to show what was needed to fix the problem, but it would never be a way for Israel to change who they were. A force much greater than willpower or good intentions would be required to restore humanity and fix the worship problem. God himself would be the one to bring it to pass. In Exodus 30, after the blessings and curses, God points to a day in the future where he will make it possible for true worship to occur.

"And when all these things come upon you, the blessing and the curse, which I have set before you, and you call them to mind among all the nations where the LORD your God has driven you, and return to the LORD your God, you and your children, and obey his voice in all that I command you today, with all your heart and with all your soul, then the LORD your God will restore your fortunes and have mercy on you, and he will gather you again from all the peoples where the LORD your God has scattered you. If your outcasts are in the uttermost parts of heaven, from there the LORD your God will gather you, and from there he will take you. And the LORD your God will bring you into the land that your fathers possessed, that you may possess it. And he will make you more prosperous and numerous than your fathers. And the LORD your God will circumcise your heart and the heart of your offspring, so that you will love the LORD your God with all your heart and with all your soul, that you may live. (Deuteronomy 30:1–6)

God was going to circumcise the hearts of his people, and somehow he was going to act in a way to bring his people back into true worship.

Jesus, through his incarnation and life, became the perfect Israelite. The one who would faithfully fulfill all the requirements of the law and unlock all of God's blessings through his obedience. The heart of Jesus and the reason he came was to fulfill this purpose. Jesus was the second Adam, the fulfillment of God's promises to Abraham, a better Moses, and the re-creation of Israel.

Just like Adam, Jesus would be taken into the wilderness for forty days to be tempted by Satan. However, unlike Adam, Jesus would stand victorious over the devil's words of deception. In the beginning, the serpent questioned the words of God. In Jesus, the serpent spoke directly to the living Word of God himself. His attempts to deceive proved laughable and futile. Jesus, through his obedience to the law, provided the means for his people to enjoy worship once again. We don't have renewed access to God through our obedience to the law. It came through the perfect obedience of Jesus.

Paul explains our relationship to the law and Jesus like this. We were faithless and disobedient to the commands of God, given through the law, and therefore placed under the curse that came from Adam's disobedience in the Garden. Jesus, as the second Adam and the re-creation of Israel, was faithful and obedient to the law. Submitting himself to the will of God the father, even though he was God himself, so that the blessings of obedience might be unlocked for those who now believe through faith in him. In short, our faith in the faithfulness of Jesus unlocks the blessing of God and gives us the ability to worship once again.

Therefore, as one trespass led to condemnation for all men, so one act of righteousness leads to justification and life for all men. For as by the one man's disobedience the many were made sinners, so by the one man's obedience the many will be made righteous. Now the law came in to increase the trespass, but where sin increased, grace abounded all the more, so that, as sin reigned in death, grace also might reign through righteousness leading to eternal life through Jesus Christ our Lord. (Romans 5:18–21)

I love how the old hymn "The Solid Rock"[5] puts it:

My hope is built on nothing less

Than Jesus' blood and righteousness

I dare not trust the sweetest frame

But wholly lean on Jesus name

On Christ the solid rock I stand

All other ground is sinking sand.

How amazing are the plans of God? How beautiful is his faithfulness? Our way back to worship is by having faith in the faithfulness of Jesus. He has done all the work, he has fulfilled the law, he has provided a way back into worship. Paul writes that "all have sinned," meaning we are all incapable of fixing the worship problem. But now, through faith in Jesus, we have been offered a way to have our brokenness and sin forgiven and taken away. Worship is restored through Jesus and Jesus alone.

Now, in our lives, the call to restored worship is found in this call to faith in Jesus. Our submission and surrender are to center on him and his work. He has done what we cannot do. He has fulfilled the law that we could not obey, and in doing so, he has removed the curse that was brought upon us by our disobedience. He is the solution to the worship problem.

---

[5] Edward Mote, "The Solid Rock," 1834.

Do you have faith in Jesus? Have you surrendered your life to him in totality? Faith is not a simple affirmation of who he is—it is a wholesale rejection of who we are and a surrender to him as king of our lives. Just as Jesus's faithfulness and submission marked the way to be forgiven and ushered in the return of true worship, our worship is now renewed by submission to Jesus and by placing our faith in his work on the cross and the power of his resurrection. He is the answer to the worship problem, and by faithfully fulfilling the law that we could not, he is the way back into the perfect worship of the Garden.

Chapter 15

Failure to Kill False Worship

———

When God gave Israel the law, he knew that it wouldn't bring their hearts back to him in worship. It would only serve as the means to magnify the worship problem that had overwhelmed the human heart. Instead of moving toward the image of the God they had rejected in the beginning, Israel would become more and more enamored with the false gods that surrounded them as they moved into the Promised Land.

As the curtain falls on the life of Moses, we find Israel ready to move into the land promised by God, led by a great warrior named Joshua. God once again promises to be faithful to Israel. He tells them to be courageous as they take possession of their new home because he will fight the battles on their behalf. This ragtag group of former slaves who had wandered in the wilderness for forty years were about to be ushered into a brand-new life because of God's commitment to his promises. They later respond to this kindness by rejecting his law and ignoring his commands to clear the new land of false worship.

As Israel prepares to claim what has been promised, they are given specific instructions on what to do once the land is theirs.

But in the cities of these peoples that the LORD your God is giving you for an inheritance, you shall save alive nothing that breathes, but you shall devote them to complete destruction, the Hittites and the Amorites, the Canaanites and the Perizzites, the Hivites and the Jebusites, as the LORD your God has commanded, that they may not teach you to do according to all their abominable practices that they have done for their gods, and so you sin against the LORD your God. (Deuteronomy 20:16–18)

God was sending his people into a land saturated with the false worship of a people known as the Canaanites, descendants of Canaan, who was the son of Ham and grandson of Noah. Canaan was cursed after Ham saw his father Noah naked in his tent, restarting the cycle of the worship problem directly on the heels of the worldwide flood. As Canaan's descendants moved further away from the heart of God, their nation expanded and permeated the earth with corruption and debauchery. God was sending his newly liberated people to crush this legacy of false worship. He sent them to claim land meant to be used as a place of restored relationship.

God's command to wipe the people of Canaan off the face of the earth doesn't come because God is a bloodthirsty tyrant. God was working to restore the worship that was lost in the Garden of Eden. Since the beginning, he had been fighting against the worship problem. The Canaanites, through their wholesale rejection of worship and submission, had led the world down a path of darkness and rebellion. If worship was to be restored for Israel to enjoy, the worship of the Canaanites had to be destroyed once and for all. This is Israel's mission as they're sent into the land of Canaan to claim the promises of God. But they don't do what God asked of them. Once again, the nation is faithless.

A long time ago, when I was living in my first house, I needed to mulch my flower beds. Through neglect, weeds had overtaken them entirely, and they looked horrible. Being a newbie in the world of landscaping, I made a terrible error. Instead of removing the weeds, I used the grass trimmer to cut them down and then simply mulched over them. You know what happened. I spent a lot of money on new mulch that just a couple of weeks later was full of weeds again. Why? Because I didn't do the work that was required to remove the problem before putting the new mulch into place. Israel's failure in their new home mirrors my mistakes in the front yard.

Judges begins with a stark statement about Israel's failure to remove the false worship of the Canaanites from their midst. The first chapter names the tribes of Israel and gives a rebuke because of their failure to drive out the people of the land as God had commanded. Because of this failure, God makes a statement that would define worship in Israel for the rest of the Old Testament.

Now the angel of the LORD went up from Gilgal to Bochim. And he said, "I brought you up from Egypt and brought you into the land that I swore to give to your fathers. I said, 'I will never break my covenant with you, and you shall make no covenant with the inhabitants of this land; you shall break down their altars.' But you have not obeyed my voice. What is this you have done? So now I say, I will not drive them out before you, but they shall become thorns in your sides, and their gods shall be a snare to you." As soon as the angel of the LORD spoke these words to all the people of Israel, the people lifted up their voices and wept. And they called the name of that place Bochim. And they sacrificed there to the LORD. (Judges 2:1–5)

Notice what is at play in this passage. First, God once again reminds his people of his faithfulness to do what he has promised to do. Any hope Israel has and any good thing that has come to them has always been because God keeps his promises. Second, Israel had once again failed to do what they had promised to do in return. God had given them the land promised to Abraham. In return, they hadn't surrendered to the will of God; they hadn't driven out the Canaanites. Because of this, the worship problem, which had been with them since the beginning, would always keep them away from the heart of God. God says of the Canaanites to Israel, "They shall become thorns in your sides, and their gods shall be a snare to you."

Failure to drive out the Canaanites was never an issue of eviction or taking someone's home away from them. It wasn't a nationalistic exercise to give to one group what belonged to another. The reason God wanted the Canaanites driven out of the land was because of their worship—he didn't want their gods to ensnare his people. To make a place where heaven and earth could commune in worship first required that false worship and false gods be silenced and removed. God's heart in rescuing his people from Egypt was to make for himself a nation set apart to once again worship him in surrender and sacrifice.

Israel's failure to do what they had been asked would have disastrous consequences and lead them down a path away from the heart of God and toward the worship of the Canaanites. Instead of lives of surrender and sacrifice, Judges tells a story of a people who fall deeper and deeper into selfishness and depravity. The last two stories in Judges are blood-chilling reminders of what happens when people reject the worship of God and put themselves at the center. Stories of murder, rape, and kidnapping illustrate what great snares the worship of the Canaanites became for Israel. In spite of all that God had done for them—freeing them from Egypt and working wonders in the wilderness—the worship problem only grew. Judges ends with the statement:

In those days there was no king in Israel. Everyone did what was right in his own eyes. (Judges 21:25)

The worship problem is on full display in this statement. If the mark of true worship is surrender and sacrifice, the opposite would be a people driven to anarchy by the desire to please themselves. God cannot be worshipped when the statement in Judges 21:25 is a reality.

On the way to school every day, my daughters and I read a psalm together (I don't read—I just drive). A few days ago, we were talking about the things we fail to eliminate from our lives that affect our worship of God. Like the Canaanites of old, we allow things to live around us that call our hearts toward other gods. David wrote a psalm about this very idea.

I will sing of steadfast love and justice;
to you, O LORD, I will make music.
I will ponder the way that is blameless.
Oh when will you come to me?
I will walk with integrity of heart
within my house;
I will not set before my eyes
anything that is worthless.
I hate the work of those who fall away;
it shall not cling to me.
A perverse heart shall be far from me;
I will know nothing of evil.

Whoever slanders his neighbor secretly
I will destroy.
Whoever has a haughty look and an arrogant heart

I will not endure.

I will look with favor on the faithful in the land,
that they may dwell with me;
he who walks in the way that is blameless
shall minister to me.

No one who practices deceit
shall dwell in my house;
no one who utters lies
shall continue before my eyes.

Morning by morning I will destroy
all the wicked in the land,
cutting off all the evildoers
from the city of the LORD." (Psalm 101)

Do you see how this psalm is about worship? David starts by saying that his life will be marked by songs about the faithfulness and justice of God. But notice what David's actions of sacrifice and surrender are in the light of his worship. He makes a wholesale attack against the things in his life that would challenge the truth of God's character. He says that he will not put before his eyes worthless things and that he will drive out the wicked, and he vows that no one who does these things will be welcome in his house.

After we read this psalm, the conversation in the car was interesting. I asked my girls, "What's a way we invite people into our house to teach us about worship?" The conversation quickly turned to social media and entertainment. Every time we open our phone or turn on our televisions, we invite people into our house to counsel us and teach us about worship. Many in the church have become like Israel as they enter the land of Canaan. They are happy to receive and ask for God's blessings, but they are quick to sit and engage with any kind of media available to them. We binge-watch shows filled with images of sex and violence—shows scripted with speech bloated with the false worship and idolatry that has existed since the beginning—while simultaneously claiming to be worshippers of God. We imagine ourselves to be more sophisticated and educated than the Israelites while at the same time falling into the same snares that they did in the Old Testament.

Are there areas of your life where you haven't driven out the images and sounds of false worship? Are you committed to guarding your house like David in a way that will not even let the worthless things of the world have an audience? Your worship hinges on your answer to this question. We cannot pretend that we are worshippers of God corporately while engaging with false gods throughout the week in the privacy of our homes.

Worship must be marked by surrender and sacrifice, a willingness to lay down whatever pushes against true worship. We haven't been called to make physical war against a flesh-and-blood enemy but spiritual war against those things that pull our hearts away. Paul says as much to the church at Corinth.

For though we walk in the flesh, we are not waging war according to the flesh. For the weapons of our warfare are not of the flesh but have divine power to destroy strongholds. We destroy arguments and every lofty opinion raised against the knowledge of God, and take every thought captive to obey Christ, being ready to punish every disobedience, when your obedience is complete. (2 Corinthians 10:3–6)

We are not at war with the armies of the Canaanites, but in a very real way, we are still driving out the worship that the world inherited from them long ago. Our commitment to this fight will determine whether or not we will worship in the intimacy and power we were created to enjoy. Our failure will result in half-hearted worship that may resemble a life connected to the heart of God but that in reality is still silent and cold, lying dormant from the effects of the worship problem.

As the Israelites move out of the time of the judges, their desire to look and sound like the surrounding nations will lead them further down paths of false worship. Had their passion been to look and sound like the God who created them, the story would have unfolded differently. What is our desire today? Will we, like the Israelites, do whatever is right in our own eyes, or will we live in surrender and sacrifice? Will we drive out the false worship that surrounds us to find ourselves face-to-face with our creator in worship?

Chapter 16

The Reflections of a King

_____

We all fall into the trap of wanting to look and sound like the people around us. When I was a kid, Hammer pants (look them up) and mullets were all the rage. Generations are defined by the looks and sounds of the decade. Polyester suits in the '70s. Hair metal in the '80s. The list goes back as far as recorded history. And while our propensity to copy the current fashion and music isn't an indicator of spiritual health, it does reveal the profound truth that we are wired to want what the culture around us says we need to have.

Over the past few decades, what is considered normal, acceptable behavior has morphed drastically. When Elvis Presley performed "Hound Dog" on *The Milton Berle Show* in June 1956, the world was on fire over the "vulgarity" of his movements onstage. Headlines that read "Beware Elvis Presley" shot to press in publications worldwide. Fast forward to 2008 when Katy Perry sang, "I kissed a girl, and I liked it," the culture hardly batted an eye. As society evolves, the church has always been prone to evolve along with it. If we aren't careful, we will allow the culture around us to define the parameters of worship. We will fall into the same trap that Israel had fallen into by the end of Judges.

The time of the judges ends with Israel doing "what was right in their own eyes," a statement that is the antithesis of true worship. If worship is marked by surrender and sacrifice, Israel was marked by egotism and self-centeredness. This is the world into which the kings of Israel were born.

God had led Israel faithfully through the years of wandering in the wilderness. He had fed them manna from heaven and given water from a rock. He had defeated stronger, more powerful nations before them. God had established himself over and over as the one Israel could follow and depend on to lead them faithfully toward his promises. However, Israel wasn't satisfied with this arrangement.

Israel wanted a king. For years God had acted as their provider, protector, and sovereign. Still, in the face of mounting pressure from rival nations and the innate human desire to look and sound like everyone around them, Israel wanted a change. They didn't want God as their king any longer—they wanted a king made of flesh and blood. The prophet Samuel begged them to reconsider. He told them a king would tax them, oppress them, force them to work for his pleasure, and take their sons off to war. The people weren't swayed. They wanted a king in the flesh, so that is what God would provide.

In 1 Samuel, we meet a man named Saul who is everything the people wanted and more—tall, athletic, and handsome. If anyone was in the market for a king and Saul walked in, the search would always be over. He was king material—or so they thought. Saul proved to be a reflection of the people themselves. Just like Israel, he was brash, prideful, arrogant, and quick to make hasty decisions with lasting consequences. In looking for a human king, what the people really wanted was to see themselves on the throne. God was rejected; Saul was raised.

Human kings would ultimately be Israel's undoing. The worship problem would now find its way into power and seated on a throne. Israel's kings would mirror who they actually were and the kind of worship they had always wanted.

It is a phenomenon of human history that rulers tend to mirror their people. After World War I, Germans were licking their wounds from a rousing defeat and simmering with anger over perceived slights on the world stage. This sense of pride and a deep desire for nationalism gave birth to Adolf Hitler. On the flip side, a fledgling nation in the late 1700s found in George Washington a leader full of humility and grace. The society that birthed his position, however, had been shaped and molded by the Great Awakening, a spirit-fueled movement that had led an entire populous to repentance and the gospel. Leaders don't define the morality and worship of a people—they are a reflection of it.

In this light, Israel found themselves staring right back at themselves in the person of Saul. His selfishness and lack of any respect for the worship of God perfectly represented the new nation of Israel. Saul's worship accentuated the entire nation's worship problem. Because of Saul's worship, God eventually removed the kingdom from his hands and gave it to another.

In 1 Samuel 13, Saul has just led the armies of Israel in victory over the armies of the Philistines. Instead of waiting for the prophet Samuel to make sacrifices to the Lord, as he had been instructed, Saul decided to make the sacrifices himself. With no regard to God's command or the true nature of worship, Saul forged ahead on his own. Just like Cain, Saul rejected God's instructions and brought a sacrifice based on himself, and just like Cain, God's action was swift. Samuel arrived and told Saul that the kingdom would be removed from his hands and given to another. In time, Saul was killed on the battlefield with his own sword, and his kingdom was given to a man named David, who we will discuss in the next chapter.

Who are the kings we have set up in our lives against the true king of the universe? Have we bowed before rulers who look and sound like we do in an attempt to find our image on the throne of our worship? Modern-day Sauls abound in the church—leaders who position themselves as God's mouthpiece but who are only interested in proclaiming themselves. Like Saul, they are handsome, wealthy, and well-spoken. Like Saul, they garner large followings with ease. But also like Saul, many of these leaders are miles away from the heart of God. We are wired to flock to these people. We see in them what we long for in ourselves. Power, prestige, and honor. May we only give our allegiance to the one true king as we seek to honor him with the sacrifice and surrender of true worship.

If leaders are a reflection of their people, then the solution cannot be found in new leadership; it must be found in new people. God knew this would be the case. After ages of flesh-and-blood kings leading his people toward destruction, God did the unthinkable. John 1 tells us that the Word became flesh and dwelt among us. The king of heaven became a king of flesh and blood. Jesus was not a reflection of the people; he was a reflection of the Father. To look at him was to see the perfection of the kingdom of heaven.

Or, as John wrote in the first chapter of his gospel, "We have seen his glory, glory as of the only Son from the Father, full of grace and truth." (John 1:14) To look upon him is to be changed into his image. To pledge allegiance to his kingdom is to find security and hope. To walk in his footsteps is to see the world set on fire with the hope of his promises. Instead of bowing to kings that resemble our forms of worship, we are now invited to surrender and sacrifice to one who can remake us into his image. Worship is restored through the kingship of Jesus Christ.

Chapter 17

The Worship of King David

If the first king of Israel was a stunning picture of everything God had never intended for his people, his choice for their second king was the opposite. No one in the Old Testament personified the worship God desired like the second king of Israel. Described as "a man after God's own heart," King David was one of Israel's only kings to genuinely seek to know God in worship. His life stands out like a flame in the midst of complete darkness compared to Israel's failed leadership.

Even David's life, however, was marred by false worship. For all his desire to worship God in truth, he was still plagued with the worship problem that lives inside each of us. The greatest king Israel would ever know wouldn't be able to bring his people back to true worship.

The life of David held all the adventure of an action movie. The story of David and Goliath appeals to both children and adults as an illustration of how the little guy can take out the big scary enemy through courage and determination. But David's heart of worship wasn't born of these ingredients. They were born of a spirit of surrender and trust. Many teachers have made the story of David and Goliath about bravery and self-assurance, but the Bible paints a different picture. David's courage was found in his faith and demonstrated through worship. He didn't trust in his power—he leaned into God's. As the giant Goliath taunts the entire army of Israel, David responds with stories of God's faithfulness rather than arrogance.

And David said, "The LORD who delivered me from the paw of the lion and from the paw of the bear will deliver me from the hand of this Philistine." (1 Samuel 17:37)

David's life would be a signpost for this sentiment—that the goodness and faithfulness of God would ultimately defeat Israel's enemies. David believed God's promises and centered his life in response. David's worship was accepted and magnified not because of his faithfulness but because of his belief in God's.

As biblical stories go, David's is one of the longer narratives in the entire Bible. We know more about him and his life than almost any other character in the scriptures. Interestingly, we find in David's life a microcosm of the entire story of the Bible. We see a life set apart by God that leads to blessing and intimacy. David is given the throne of Israel and the favor of God based on his desire to worship in truth.

But as the story continues, we see a shift, just like in the Garden of Eden. David begins to believe that he is great in himself. He commits horrible atrocities that affect entire families and generations for years to come. David's story is the human story. But God is faithful.

Even amid David's unfaithfulness, God once again makes promises. In a reiteration of his promises, God speaks to David through the prophet Nathan and tells him that he will establish his throne forever. That one will come after him who will rule on an eternal throne over the people of God. Just as God had promised Abraham, he spoke to David similar things.

When your days are fulfilled and you lie down with your fathers, I will raise up your offspring after you, who shall come from your body, and I will establish his kingdom. He shall build a house for my name, and I will establish the throne of his kingdom forever. I will be to him a father, and he shall be to me a son. (2 Samuel 7:12–14)

David had many sons, the most famous being Solomon who would come into power after his death. None of these sons were the ones God was speaking of. The offspring to come from David who would rule eternally would be Jesus. David foreshadowed the eternal king who was to come. In studying his life, we see the posture of worship that God had been longing for from his people since the Fall.

David's life was soap opera material. After defeating Goliath, David went back to tending sheep, but not for long. King Saul was tormented by an evil spirit that corrupted his mind and plunged his life into darkness. Music was a balm that put Saul at peace, and David was a skilled musician. In a twist of irony, the one who had been anointed as Saul's replacement was brought into the throne room to play therapeutically for God's soon-to-be deposed king. David faithfully served the man who sat on the throne that had now been promised to him. Already in David's life, we see elements of sacrifice and surrender. He was content to let God determine his destiny. He was happy to serve even as that service brought him hardship and danger. Saul attempted to kill David multiple times because of his torment, but David wouldn't reciprocate. His life was a picture of surrender to the will of God.

Later, David ran from Saul, hiding in the wilderness to preserve his life. On two separate occasions, David had the opportunity to take Saul's life and seize the throne promised to him. David refuses both opportunities. Unlike Abraham and Sarah, who took the promises of God into their own hands, David is patient and waits for the Lord to move on his behalf. His response to the opportunity to kill Saul is beautiful.

The LORD forbid that I should put out my hand against the LORD's anointed." (1 Samuel 26:11)

David realized that it was God who set up kings and removed them from power. He was content to trust God and wait for his promises to come to fruition. Often worship demands that we wait on the promises of God. Waiting is a crucial ingredient to submission. God will always come through on promises but will at times make us lean into faith to know him on a deeper level. In the waiting, our worship is expressed in the most potent ways, even when the outcome is different from what we expected.

A few years ago, my family flew to China to adopt a little girl we named Josie Rose. Josie is a derivative of the Hebrew name Joseph, which means, "May the Lord give increase." Our prayer for her has always been that her life would be a catalyst of faith for those around her. In her short life, she has already lived a deeper story than most will in a lifetime. Josie was found on the side of a busy street in Nanjing with a note pinned to her shirt that read, "We are very poor. Her mother has a very bad cancer. We hope someone can save her life."

Josie was born with multiple major heart defects, and in China, the poor aren't able to pay for health care. Her birth parents' only choice to save her life was to abandon her in the hope that the state would give her care. After a temporary surgery provided enough oxygen to keep her alive, our family showed up to bring her home when she was just eighteen months old.

Upon our arrival back in the States, Josie was immediately prepared for major heart surgery at Vanderbilt University Medical Center in Nashville, Tennessee. The day of her surgery was one of the longest of my life. Her tiny body was on bypass for hours as the doctors worked to repair all the missing pieces in her tiny heart.

After surgery, I discovered that witnessing her recovery was even harder than the waiting. Multiple machines and trees of IV medications surrounded her in the intensive care unit. After days and days, we could finally take her home. Before we left, one of the doctors sat us down and delivered hard news. While the surgery was successful, it wasn't perfect. Her heart was still in distress.

She would need more surgeries. Josie's life still hung in the balance. I will never forget the long drive from Nashville home to Knoxville. Josie sat in pain, trying to find comfort from the wound in her chest. My wife, Emily, and I sat in silence and cried. Why had God brought us all the way to China only to not come through in the surgery? Why was obedience causing so much pain? Shouldn't the promises of God equal rainbows and butterflies instead? We were learning what David found as he ran for his life, dodging the rage of a crazed king. God's promises always come true but rarely how we think they will.

I will never forget holding Josie in her room as she cried in pain, listening to the words of the song, "Tis So Sweet to Trust in Jesus."[6]

Yes, 'tis sweet to trust in Jesus
Just from sin and self to cease
Just from Jesus simply taking

---

[6] Louisa M. R. Stead, "Tis So Sweet to Trust in Jesus," 1882.

Life and rest and joy and peace.

Hot tears ran down my face as we swayed to the beautiful melody of the song. The promises of God weren't wrapped up in whether or not we live or die. God could use my life and Josie's through any situation to give increase. My job through the worship of my life was to surrender to the story he wanted to tell. God was good. He was present. He was faithful.

Josie recovered from her surgery, and upon recheck, the doctors found her heart had healed beyond expectations. No more surgeries would be required in the immediate future. If you ever meet her, you will marvel at the story God is telling through her life, but he could have also told the same through her death. The same is true of you and me.

David's worship was wired and fueled by this truth—God is in control. Our job is to surrender and sacrifice. We do not run ahead of his promises. We do not substitute our plans for his. Our mission is to worship.

However, David wasn't immune to the effects of the worship problem. Saul was eventually killed on the battlefield, and after some political turmoil, David took the throne. God blessed the nation of Israel under David's rule and, in turn, blessed David himself. He was no longer running for his life in the wilderness. He was living in a palace in Jerusalem.

We push against the seasons of wilderness in our lives, yet they are the places of growth. When things are easy, faith tends to weaken. I have heard it said many times—and know it to be true myself—that not much grows on mountaintops. The view is beautiful, but life is scarce. Real growth happens in the valley, where hard things happen, where Jesus comes to sit and eat meals with us in the middle of our battles. David's life was no different. One of the most tragic passages in the Bible comes as David is walking in ease on the roof of his palace.

In the spring of the year, the time when kings go out to battle, David sent Joab, and his servants with him, and all Israel. And they ravaged the Ammonites and besieged Rabbah. But David remained at Jerusalem. It happened, late one afternoon, when David arose from his couch and was walking on the roof of the king's house, that he saw from the roof a woman bathing; and the woman was very beautiful. (2 Samuel 11:1–2)

David was meant to be out in the heat of the fight but had decided to stay home. The beautiful woman he saw bathing, Bathsheba, was the wife of another man, but David didn't care. He was a powerful king; he could do whatever he wanted. He sent for her, slept with her, and sent her away pregnant. When he discovered the pregnancy, instead of confession, David turned to more deceit. He had her husband killed in battle and brought Bathsheba into the palace as his own wife. The heart of the boy who fought Goliath based on the faithfulness of God was now living in the darkness of the worship problem.

Nathan, the prophet who had spoken God's promises over David, was sent to deliver his judgment. The child died. David's family was plunged into chaos. Later, his son Amnon raped his daughter Tamar. His oldest son, Absalom, then killed Amnon out of rage at the act. David's sin echoed through his family's story. Absalom eventually staged a coup and took the throne from David. In a shameful act of power, he set up a tent on his father's house in full view of the people of Israel and raped his father's concubines. David's sin reverberated darkness that affected Israel's kings for generations to come. The shepherd who had become a king found himself once again running for his life and hiding in the wilderness —this time from his own son.

You may be wondering, "Why is this guy called a man after God's own heart?" An excellent question with an even greater answer. There is actually so much hope to be found in the story of David's downfall. It comes because of his repentance. David returns to a posture of worship and confesses his sins to God. He recognizes his unfaithfulness and pleads for God to remember his. Here is where we see the heart of God on display for us through the life of David.

When you read Psalms, they are full of David's life. He is the author of around half the songs found there. Although most of us like to read the happy ones, a majority are laments—confessions of sin that highlight the need for God's forgiveness and faithfulness. One of David's most famous confessions was written after he committed adultery and murder.

Have mercy on me, O God,

according to your steadfast love;

according to your abundant mercy

blot out my transgressions.

Wash me thoroughly from my iniquity,

and cleanse me from my sin! (Psalm 51:1–2)

Another he wrote as he ran from Absalom after his son usurped his throne.

O LORD, how many are my foes!

Many are rising against me;

many are saying of my soul,

"There is no salvation for him in God."

But you, O LORD, are a shield about me,

my glory, and the lifter of my head.

I cried aloud to the LORD,

and he answered me from his holy hill. (Psalm 3:1–4)

No matter what we have done and despite the consequences of our actions, God longs to forgive us and display his love and mercy. The Bible is a story about a faithful God who loves an unfaithful people. My life is the same story, as is yours. Not even adultery, deceit, or murder can erase or disqualify us from the promises of

God. The responses of sacrifice and surrender to his kindness are always available to those who will kneel in worship.

I love the psalms for this reason. I encourage you to spend some significant time there. Through them, we come in contact with the raw everyday reality of the worship problem. They aren't happy truisms about the love of God. They are filled with real-life struggles of people painfully aware that life is broken and marred by sin—people who cling to the promise that the only hope for a solution to the worship problem is the kindness and faithfulness of God. Psalms served as the songbook for Israel's worship—the hottest singles of the day—and they were real. David put his innermost struggles on full display as he poured out his heart in worship. How amazing that God invites the reality of our brokenness into spaces created for worship. He doesn't ask us to act like we are something we aren't; he calls us to bring all the broken pieces and lay them down in an act of surrender.

David's life ends, and after some political turmoil, the throne passes to his son Solomon. David's life shows us once again that no matter how righteous a person may be, the worship problem prevents them from being the solution to the Fall. Not even the greatest king can rule over the rebellion of our hearts. God would be the one to bring the darkness into submission.

As Jesus hung on the cross, his Roman executioners fashioned a crude sign that read, "King of the Jews." The promises of God don't usually match our expectations, but they always come to fruition in the end.

Chapter 18

Tabernacle and Temple Worship

Israel's worship took more explicit form in the wilderness as God commanded them to build a special place for worship. Eden had been the place where heaven and earth came together as one, the place of overlap where things made of flesh and those made of spirit collided. Just as God had walked among his creation in the Garden of Eden, he then made a way to do the same among Israel through the tabernacle and the temple. He had freed Israel from Egypt for this purpose. He had always wanted to return to the start and be with them, even as they continually ran in the other direction. God said this exact thing to Moses.

I will make my dwelling among you, and my soul shall not abhor you. And I will walk among you and will be your God, and you shall be my people. I am the LORD your God, who brought you out of the land of Egypt, that you should not be their slaves. (Leviticus 26:11–13)

The first iteration of this unique space was the tabernacle, a tent that could be packed up and moved as the people wandered in the wilderness. Later, once Solomon became king of Israel, a permanent structure was erected in its place. In these spaces, the divine drew near to sinful people solely based on his love and his desire to be with them. In these sacred spaces, he also gave them a way to have their sins forgiven, a way to return to Eden.

Take a moment to read 1 Kings 6-7 and notice how the temple Solomon built was decorated. Flowers, pomegranates, and animals dominate the visuals in this sacred place of worship, all commissioned to resemble an outdoor space. Cedar was used throughout the temple, its aromatic power filling the space with the smells of a garden. Genesis 2:12 mentions that gold, bdellium, and onyx were prevalent in the sanctuary of Eden, all materials used in the construction of the temple.

The instruments used in the temple ceremonies also took their shape from the Garden. From the lampstand shaped like a tree to the ark of the covenant, every element was crafted as a reminder of Genesis. The door of the temple faced east toward where Eden had once stood as the center of communion between God and humanity. As God's spirit rested in a temple made by hands, he was positioned toward the perfect sanctuary that had been lost. It was as if God was looking longingly from the temple door back to the rebellion that had broken his heart. The sights, smells, and sounds of temple worship would have been a way to reflect on the pain of loss while offering a way in the present to make things right again.

Rebellion had to be dealt with, and through temple worship, God gave his people a means of atonement and reconnection.

Atonement is a word used over and over again in the Bible. It carries with it the idea of making right something that was wrong or repairing something that has been broken. In humanity's case, we are what is broken; we are the source of all that is wrong. God is holy. He is distinct. He is perfect. Just like you wouldn't throw muddy clothes in the drawer with clean ones, we cannot just waltz into the presence of God in worship covered in the filth of our sin. Something had to be done to make us presentable in the courts of worship once again. As we have seen through Noah and the people of Israel, even on our best days, we aren't capable of fixing what we have shattered. This is what atonement provides—a way to have our sins forgiven. The old hymn "Jesus Paid It All" says it best, "Sin had left a crimson stain, He washed it white as snow."[7]

The highlight of the sacred ceremonies held in the temple was known as the Day of Atonement. Once a year, the high priest of Israel would enter the most sacred space of the temple, known as the holy of holies, to make sacrifices for the sins of the nation. The holy of holies was a small room separated from the rest of the temple by a heavy curtain. The curtain signified that no one was allowed to enter into that space because it was there that the spirit of God lived on earth. The holy of holies was the re-creation of Eden, the place where God dwelled with humanity.

---

[7] Lyrics by Elvina M. Hall (1865), music by John T. Grape (1868).

It was not out of exclusion that people couldn't enter into the holy of holies; it was out of kindness. To enter into the presence of God as a sinner would mean instant death. God's holiness and glory would crush anyone who came into his presence under the darkness of their sins. But the holy of holies was also the place where the sins of the people could be atoned for, where their darkness could be transformed into light once again.

Within the holy of holies stood the ark of the covenant, a special box God had commanded Israel to make to serve as the center of their sacred ceremonies. In the ark, they stored the Ten Commandments and other artifacts that signified freedom from slavery and their time in the wilderness. But the lid of the ark was where the most essential work of atonement took place.

The top of the ark was known as the mercy seat. Once a year, on the Day of Atonement, the high priest threw blood from the people's sacrifices onto the mercy seat as a means of atonement for their sins. The blood of an innocent animal served as the sign of their redemption. On that day, the people gathered and worshipped as the high priest made things right between a sinful people and a holy God. In this picture, we find the work of Jesus on full display.

From the beginning, the worship problem has been one of rebellion and loss of intimacy with God. As we have seen, even as God calls his people out of slavery and into relationship, their hearts are still unable to draw near to him. In the temple, the blood of bulls and lambs served as a reminder of the deadly cost of atonement for the people's rebellion. But the atonement gained by these sacrifices was only temporary. In the New Testament, we read sacrifices were only a sign pointing toward what God was going to do in the future to atone for sins once and for all.

For since the law has but a shadow of the good things to come instead of the true form of these realities, it can never, by the same sacrifices that are continually offered every year, make perfect those who draw near. Otherwise, would they not have ceased to be offered, since the worshipers, having once been cleansed, would no longer have any consciousness of sins? But in these sacrifices there is a reminder of sins every year. For it is impossible for the blood of bulls and goats to take away sins. (Hebrews 10:1–4)

Through temple sacrifices, God drew attention to the need for something greater to atone for the rebellion that had broken worship in the beginning. He was providing language and understanding of what was to come. The entire temple system was a way to point to Jesus, who would become the ultimate sacrifice that would restore access to the presence of God.

Just as Eden and the temple were the places of connection between heaven and earth, Jesus, through his body, became the ultimate replacement of both. He made this very claim in the days leading up to his death.

So the Jews said to him, "What sign do you show us for doing these things?" Jesus answered them, "Destroy this temple, and in three days I will raise it up." The Jews then said, "It has taken forty-six years to build this temple, and will you raise it up in three days?" But he was speaking about the temple of his body. (John 2:18–21)

Do you see why this statement made the Israelite elite so angry? Jesus claimed that their holiest place was going to be destroyed and replaced with himself. To those Jewish leaders, this resounded with blasphemy. In the eyes of heaven, it was our way home. Through Jesus, we now have access to the presence of God.

The fantastic thing is that those of us now connected to Christ through salvation are part of this temple replacement in the present day. The church of Jesus Christ is now the re-created temple. We are the place where heaven and earth come together. We are meant to be the conduit of God's spirit to the earth, the place where he has come to live. A touch from you is intended to be a touch from Jesus. When someone speaks with you, they are meant to hear what heaven sounds like. Our worship has become the place where Eden works its way back into the present. Look at what Peter says:

As you come to him, a living stone rejected by men but in the sight of God chosen and precious, you yourselves like living stones are being built up as a spiritual house, to be a holy priesthood, to offer spiritual sacrifices acceptable to God through Jesus Christ. (1 Peter 2:4–5)

This is why the worship problem must be remedied. It is not just about you. God intends to use your worship to reconnect a lost world back to himself. He wants to use your response of surrender and sacrifice to connect the broken back to his heart. You are the new place God's spirit wants to live amid his creation. You are the new temple of the Holy Spirit. Through Jesus, all this has been made possible.

It gets better. Not only is Jesus the re-creation of the temple, but he is also the high priest responsible for making the sacrifices for sin. Remember, we said it was the high priest who entered the holy of holies once a year to atone for the people's rebellion. According to the book of Hebrews, Jesus has become the highest and final of high priests.

Since then we have a great high priest who has passed through the heavens, Jesus, the Son of God, let us hold fast our confession. For we do not have a high priest who is unable to sympathize with our weaknesses, but one who in every respect has been tempted as we are, yet without sin. Let us then with confidence draw near to the throne of grace, that we may receive mercy and find grace to help in time of need. (Hebrews 4:14–16)

Jesus, as the final high priest, has done so much more than any high priest could have done before him. In temple worship, the high priest could only enter the holy of holies once a year, and even then, the sacrifices weren't able to remove the brokenness of sin. Jesus has entered once and for all to remove our sin and make us fit to worship God in intimacy. In fact, at his death, as Jesus cried out into a darkened sky the beautiful words, "It is finished," the curtain in the temple, made to hide the holy of holies from public view, was torn from top to bottom, unmasking the place of atonement for the world to see. Through his death, Jesus made a way for humanity to come into the presence of God through worship.

The connection to temple worship is deeper still. Jesus has also become the mercy seat. Remember, the top of the ark of the covenant was the place of mercy in the temple. The sacred place where the blood of the sacrificed lamb was sprinkled. In Romans 3, Paul says that Jesus has now become the place of mercy for our sins. Jesus has become the place where we find forgiveness and atonement. Jesus is the perfect sacrifice for our sins. (Romans 3:21–26) He is the lamb of God that takes away the sins of the world. (John 1:29)

The system of temple worship always pointed to something in the future. Through Jesus, the world was given a way to return to the presence of God without the blood of bulls and goats. A temple is no longer necessary to have access to God because Jesus himself has become the place of mercy and worship. Since Jesus is the high priest, there is no need to seek out anyone to speak to God on your behalf. It is a fantastic thought that through Jesus, you and I can talk directly to God himself, just like in the beginning. What was lost in Eden through our rebellion has been restored to us through Jesus's faithfulness. Have you experienced this? Have you had a personal and direct conversation with God to surrender to the work of Jesus in your life?

The worship problem finds its solution through Jesus's work on the cross and the power of his resurrection. Now, instead of the blood of a lamb, all that is required to have atonement for our rebellion is surrender. He becomes the center of our confession; he becomes the place of atonement for our brokenness.

If we confess our sins, he is faithful and just to forgive us our sins and to cleanse us from all unrighteousness. (1 John 1:9)

Or as Paul writes to the church in Rome:

If you confess with your mouth that Jesus is Lord and believe in your heart that God raised him from the dead, you will be saved. (Romans 10:9)

Confess that he is Lord. Submit to him as king. He is worthy of surrender and sacrifice. He is worthy of worship. Worship is restored as Jesus is made Lord of our lives. When we bow in submission, the work of atonement—made possible by Jesus—is given to us completely. We are renewed. We are reborn. We are taken back to the Garden once again.

Just as the temple served as the center of God's desire to be united with his chosen people through worship, it would also point to the absolute corruption of the human heart. The prophet

Jeremiah, tasked with bringing words of judgment because of corrupt temple worship, wrote, "The heart is deceitful above all things, and desperately sick; who can understand it?" (Jeremiah 17:9) As the Old Testament moves toward a close, the temple becomes the center of God's broken heart. In the temple, Israel forgets the gift of his presence and replaces it with gods of their own design once again.

Chapter 19

Worship Corrupted Again

As the story of the Old Testament draws to a close, the reader is brought face-to-face with the reality that the worship problem has not been remedied. In fact, it has become a cancerous infection within God's chosen people and appears to be immovable. God sends warnings for hundreds of years through prophets who speak of impending judgment and slavery because of Israel's disobedience, but the people don't listen. They are convinced that because they are the chosen people of God, nothing bad can happen to them.

As you read the prophets, all of it should be framed in the light of corrupted worship. God's plan to be reunited with his people hadn't come to fruition. He had been rejected. However, even in their rejection of God, the people believed they were absolutely immune to consequences because surely God would never harm the temple in Jerusalem. He would never put at risk the very place in which his spirit dwelt among them. The prophet Jeremiah warned the people against this thinking.

Thus says the LORD of hosts, the God of Israel: Amend your ways and your deeds, and I will let you dwell in this place. Do not trust in these deceptive words: 'This is the temple of the LORD, the temple of the LORD, the temple of the LORD.'

"For if you truly amend your ways and your deeds, if you truly execute justice one with another, if you do not oppress the sojourner, the fatherless, or the widow, or shed innocent blood in this place, and if you do not go after other gods to your own harm, then I will let you dwell in this place, in the land that I gave of old to your fathers forever.

"Behold, you trust in deceptive words to no avail. Will you steal, murder, commit adultery, swear falsely, make offerings to Baal, and go after other gods that you have not known, and then come and stand before me in this house, which is called by my name, and say, 'We are delivered!'—only to go on doing all these abominations? Has this house, which is called by my name, become a den of robbers in your eyes? Behold, I myself have seen it, declares the LORD. (Jeremiah 7:3–11)

But Israel wouldn't listen. Not only did they mirror the Canaanite nations that surrounded them, but they also moved into deeper, darker places of worship as they sought to blend the worship of God with the religion of their own desires. On the hillsides of their cities, they worshipped the fertility goddess Asherah, recalling the golden calf worship from the wilderness.

They bowed down to Baal in offerings of surrender. They sacrificed innocent human life to the god Molech. Despite God's unwavering faithfulness, Israel only grew in unfaithfulness.

The fires on the hillsides of Israel and Judah flickered with clockwork regularity. Flames illuminated where the people in the villages below had placed their allegiance and hope. In Jerusalem, the holy city, the feet of the worshippers carried them away from the temple and up hilltops covered with wooden poles and trees adorned in honor of Asherah. They loved her immensely. Surrender and sacrifice were now given in her honor.

The worship of Yahweh God in the temple was to be marked by reverential holiness and an acknowledgment of sin. Asherah demanded carnal reverie and sexual offerings to gain favor. Yahweh dwelt with his chosen people in spirit. He had delivered his people through feats of strength and provision. He had proven his faithfulness and love over and over again. In return, he had asked to be the sole recipient of Israel's devotion and love.

The rules of the law, however, hadn't suited Israel's real desire. They fashioned new gods out of wood and gold, submitting to them in pagan rituals of unbridled sexual passion and sacrifice. On the high places won for them by Yahweh God, Israel sank into the depths. Driven into the hillside, wood became the symbol of Israel's impending slavery.

The Old Testament is littered with references to this wicked goddess and her place in the history of Israel's worship. As time progressed, she wasn't limited to just the high places but found a place in the temple of Yahweh God himself. Israel never rejected Yahweh outright—they always leaned on and maintained pride in their position as God's chosen people. They longed for and demanded his blessing. They claimed his promises through the covenants made to their forefathers. To maintain a semblance of who they were called to be, Asherah became the "wife" of Yahweh and was given a place of honor in the temple in Jerusalem. We read of her in Jeremiah.

The children gather wood, the fathers kindle fire, and the women knead dough, to make cakes for the queen of heaven. And they pour out drink offerings to other gods. (Jeremiah 7:18)

In the sacred halls constructed for worshipping the God of heaven, the people of Israel brought in the queen of their debauchery. They presented her to Yahweh as a bride. Speaking of coming judgment, the prophet Jeremiah facetiously references the people's feasts for "the queen of heaven" and the people's love and honor given to her above God himself. As God had proclaimed himself Israel's father, the broken hearts of the people gave birth to a destitute, false, and wicked mother. There were brief periods where good kings like Josiah removed Asherah from the temple and destroyed the high places. Still, as quickly as she was removed, kings like Manasseh welcomed her back into the holy places with open arms.

Modern archeological discoveries in the land of Canaan have found figurines fashioned in her likeness residing in every aspect of Israel's life. Women would hold her as they birthed children and pray for safe deliveries. Men would seek her blessing as they gave themselves to prostitutes in her honor. Families would pray for her fertility to bless them as they grew crops. Israel would soon learn the truth of the prophet Isaiah's warning—God would not share his glory with another. (Isaiah 42:8)

Asherah was not the only false god to whom Israel swore allegiance. She was joined by gods like Baal and Molech, who each demanded their own sacraments of carnal expression to gain favor and blessing. All were eventually brought into the temple of God, turning what was once a shining display of God's presence amid his people into a den of death and sexual debauchery. In a horrific display of just how far the hearts of the people had fallen into darkness, Israel's kings cut the throats of their infant sons in sacrificial fires of worship to these false deities. In the depths of their rebellion, Israel was blind to the fact that God was still crying out to be their God. He shouted warnings through the prophets of the brutal judgment on the horizon. In their darkness, Israel remained confident that they were secure as the people of God even though their actions demonstrated they had no idea who he was.

Israel's sin has never left the heart of humankind. They wanted God on their terms. They crafted their worship in a way that fulfilled their own desires, never the desires God had for them. The worship God had laid out through Moses and the law sought to change a lost and wayward people into the image of a supreme and holy God. The worship Israel made for themselves tried to turn a supreme and holy God into something small and familiar birthed out of their own desire. It seems impossible that temple prostitutes would be brought into God's sacred places so that the people could live in sexual "freedom" as they simultaneously worshipped the God who had declared his hatred of it. Rather than God, the people's hearts decided what worship should be. Whenever that is the equation, communion with God will be replaced with his judgment.

The temple, which was meant to be the connection between heaven and earth, had been corrupted by the rebellion of the Fall. We must ask ourselves whether we are guilty of the same today. In this spirit, Paul questions the church at Corinth about sexual sins in the context of their worship.

Flee from sexual immorality. Every other sin a person commits is outside the body, but the sexually immoral person sins against his own body. Or do you not know that your body is a temple of the Holy Spirit within you, whom you have from God? You are not your own, for you were bought with a price. So glorify God in your body. (1 Corinthians 6:18–20)

If we are joined together with the things of the Fall, we are no longer worshipping in surrender and sacrifice. We have re-created the sins of Israel within the temple of our own bodies. This is why holiness is vital in worship. You are meant to connect the world to God as his living temple, and that cannot happen if the place of connection is corrupted with the modern spirit of Asherah. We like to think that our modern sensibilities have changed the narrative of idolatry. Still, the reality is that Asherah has always found a way to be reborn and renamed.

Israel ended up conquered by her enemies. God burned the temple of Solomon. The holy place of worship—birthed out of his desire to once again be with his people—melted in fire, along with the false gods that had made their homes within its walls. Asherah, Baal, and Molech melted in the heat of God's demand for holiness. Israel's pride and self-dependence met the same fate.

After a long period of renewed exile and slavery, the people eventually returned in oppression to their homeland. A new temple, though smaller and less grand, was eventually built. God remained silent for four hundred years. No prophet spoke. No king led. Asherah and her lifeless compatriots faded into darkness as did Israel's hope. But God always fulfills his promises, and he never abandons his people.

As wood driven into the ground on the high places outside of Jerusalem had marked the rebellion of his chosen people, God in his goodness would take the symbol of their brokenness and use it for their redemption. Just like the Asherah poles of Israel's past, years later, another pole would find its place on the hillside outside of Jerusalem. The worshippers would once again make their way up the hillside away from the temple. Where the hearts of his chosen people had once given themselves to other gods and goddesses around wooden poles, Jesus would hang on a cross to make atonement for their sins.

As the eyes of Jesus scanned the faces of his accusers, as his heart remembered the sins of Israel's past, as his ears heard the sounds of cursing and rejection, as his flesh felt the searing pain of being nailed to the symbol of Israel's death, his voice would cry out and echo over the hills of Jerusalem, "Father, forgive them." Wood, driven into the ground, would no longer be the symbol of Israel's slavery; it would become the sign of her deliverance.

As Israel's story comes to a close, there is a striking question to ask of our own hearts in the modern church. Are we worshipping out of a desire to be made into the image of the resurrected Jesus? Or are we worshipping in a way that demands that he be made into ours? Are our lives marked by a desire for holiness and surrender? Or do we feed every carnal desire throughout the week and then declare ourselves the people of God in the darkened rooms of our worship gatherings?

We are now children of grace born of the love of God. However, grace is our freedom to be made into the image of Christ, never our excuse to stay the same. The apostle Paul writing to the church in Rome poses the question, "Are we to continue in sin that grace may abound?" The answer he gives is a resounding no! He continues by asking, "How can we who died to sin still live in it?" (Romans 6:1–2)

Worship is transformation. Worship is surrender. Worship is sacrifice. Worship is the presentation of broken people to a perfect God to become something different from what they were. Worship is never marked simply by passionate declarations of allegiance; it is marked by the gritty day-to-day act of change, sacrifice, and dying to self. Israel wanted God's promises absent from his holiness. We must not fall into the same way of thinking in our worship. Are we allowing our worship of God to change us into his image, or are we demanding that God be made into ours and setting the terms for our worship?

The Old Testament is saturated with story and metaphor that still lives in every dead cavern in the heart of man. Whereas the means of grace have changed and now find their being in Jesus, the broken places of our hearts have remained unmoved. God's heart grieved for his children in the Old Testament, just as it does now. God longed for a redeemed people who would become his chosen family and reflect his goodness. The stories about Israel prove that this could never happen through righteous men, nationalistic dreams, or the leadership of fallen kings. They needed a redeemer, a true king who could lead them back to the heart of the Father. Jesus would hang on a wooden pole, on a hill, outside of the holy city. Through the surrender and sacrifice of this king, worship would find new birth. God's people would be born again in Jesus himself.

Chapter 20

We Must Be Changed

_____

The aim of this book has been to trace the worship problem back to the start, drawing a line into the present to show the way home. There is hope. There is a future. There is a way to worship again, even though the way there is not always easy to see. The three realities of the worship problem we have seen throughout the Old Testament are:

1. We were created to worship.

2. We changed the object of our worship, which in turn changed us.

3. We now must be changed to truly worship again.

It really is that simple. In fact, the Bible is the story of these three truths. Every story you read, every line in its sacred pages, points to these realities. If we can see how these things have impacted our lives and our churches and alter our course back toward true worship, we will see the face of God and find ourselves healed.

The hard part is that altering any course is more laborious than continuing down the same path. Healing always involves change, even if that change isn't easy. Those who are sick need to be altered into those who are well. Refusing the change of healing is to stay infirmed or even die. The car that has been wrecked must be changed at the body shop to be drivable again. The life that has been ruined must be put back together to genuinely worship as it was created to. But even though change can be scary and daunting, take hope in this fact: the change needed for you to become a worshipper once again is not something you have to do on your own. As a matter of fact, it isn't something you can do on your own even if you wanted to.

Jesus, through his love, will be the one to change you. Your only job in the equation is to surrender and let him. It won't be easy. Allowing Jesus to change us isn't always pleasant. But if you are willing to be altered by his love and grace, you will find yourself living for the first time as you were meant to—as a true worshipper of God.

Even as you read this, some will want the change that Jesus offers while at the same time rejecting it out of hand. We know that what we have been doing has brought nothing but pain and failure. Still, the thought of surrendering our lives to another is terrifying. Why is change so hard? Why do we long to be made into something different while at the same time revolting against the very thing that offers to give us what we know we need? The answer is simple and is actually the reason we ran away from God in the first place. We don't want anyone telling us how or what we are supposed to worship. The core of the human heart is the desire to decide what, where, who, and how we will worship. To allow someone else to dictate who we will be goes against the very nature of who we have become.

Human history and nature in this reality cannot be denied. Humanity's desire to dictate the terms of our worship can be summed up by the famous poem "Invictus" by William Ernest Henley.

Out of the night that covers me,
　　Black as the pit from pole to pole,
I thank whatever gods may be
　　For my unconquerable soul.
In the fell clutch of circumstance
　　I have not winced nor cried aloud.
Under the bludgeonings of chance
　　My head is bloody, but unbowed.
Beyond this place of wrath and tears
　　Looms but the Horror of the shade,
And yet the menace of the years
　　Finds and shall find me unafraid.
It matters not how strait the gate,
　　How charged with punishments the scroll,
I am the master of my fate,
　　I am the captain of my soul.

Children recite a shorter version of this poem every day to their parents: "You can't tell me what to do!" Yet to find ourselves healed and whole, this mantra must be changed. The sentiment of this poem cannot stand if the worship problem is to be solved.

God will not be worshipped on our terms—he demands that we come to him on his. This demand is not wrapped in cold egotism; rather, God knows who and what we were created to be. A car wouldn't do well trying to be a boat, and a boat can't function on the hard reality of the interstate. In the same way, we find our lives in an endless loop of futility when we attempt to determine our worship. Yet God, in his patience, waits for us to surrender to find ourselves healed and whole.

Worship cannot be restored on our terms or in the world we have built—it must be discovered as we leave the faraway lands to which we have wandered. Through the surrender of true worship, we must chart a course back home. Like Abraham, God calls us to leave the things we have built in order to have the kingdom he is building. For ages, preachers have thundered the mantra of asking Jesus into your heart. While well intended, this phrase is misleading. The return to worship isn't asking Jesus into your heart —it's Jesus inviting you into his.

This surrender is hard. From childhood, we live our lives focused on who we are and what we want to be when we grow up. We live in ongoing confusion as we continue down this path of perceived autonomy, choosing careers and spouses based on our personal goals and needs. We then scratch our heads and wonder why none of our plans have ended in happiness. We think to ourselves, "Maybe I just need more stuff to go along with the plan." We scratch and claw to have more and bigger and better of the same stuff we already have stored in the garage and then are dumbfounded when none of it seems to work.

After all of this, we hear of Jesus. He can fix it! So we ask Jesus to come in and clean up our mess. "Arrange all this stuff," we tell him. "Order the chaos of my life." The problem is that Jesus actually offers something better and harder in the call of the gospel. He hasn't come to fix what we have built and broken—he asks us to leave them behind. Let's read what Jesus said in Luke 9 one more time.

And he said to all, "If anyone would come after me, let him deny himself and take up his cross daily and follow me. For whoever would save his life will lose it, but whoever loses his life for my sake will save it. For what does it profit a man if he gains the whole world and loses or forfeits himself? (Luke 9:23–25)

Do you see what Jesus is saying? What we often ask him to do is come into the shoddy heart kingdoms and cities that we have built. We point to all the broken-down buildings and ask him to fix up the place. We basically ask Jesus to become the maintenance man in the broken worship slums of our own making. We intend to maintain control of what gets built and where, but maybe Jesus can put a little sparkle on it afterward.

Jesus offers something entirely different. Jesus takes one look at the dilapidated condition of the kingdoms we have crafted and holds out a book of matches. He says that to have him, we have to burn our slums and kingdoms to the ground, leave them behind, and follow him to the kingdom he is building. In fact, this will be the mantra of his entire ministry.

Jesus came into Galilee, proclaiming the gospel of God, and saying, "The time is fulfilled, and the kingdom of God is at hand; repent and believe in the gospel." (Mark 1:14–15)

The good news of God requires that we leave our old broken-down kingdoms to have the shiny new kingdom that Jesus is building. In this offer from Jesus, we find the core of our worship problem. We have never wanted to do this. We have always wanted Jesus to come into our kingdom instead of leaving the safety of what we have built in order to enter his. But only when we leave these places will we see the promises of God spring to life.

Since the day the sanctuary of Eden was lost, we have been churning out false gods that seem more acceptable to who we are and who we want to be. We live to give our time, money, talents, and allegiance to them. We have seen, through Israel's story, that these gods have always been the same. Their names and faces have changed, but at their core, they are as present now as they have ever been. We worship them because we love ourselves, and in them, we find the things we think will make us happy and whole. But just like my friend Jeff, we are left empty-handed and confused as they fail to deliver on what our worship of them promised. All of human experience bears out this truth. John Calvin famously wrote, "The human mind is, so to speak, a perpetual forge of idols."[8] Put another way, your heart is an idol factory, churning out false gods at an alarming rate. If you are honest with yourself, you will realize that your life is a stunning affirmation of this reality.

As our hearts long to see Jesus and know God through worship restored, the solution lies in the work of Jesus and our willingness to let him change us. We must be changed! Surrender and sacrifice must drive our lives. As we lose our lives for the sake of Jesus, we will find a new life that is actually the one we were meant to live.

---

[8] John Calvin, *Institutes of the Christian Religion*, trans. Henry Beveridge (Grand Rapids: Christian Classics Ethereal Library, 1845), 97.

Chapter 21

Worship in the End

My birth state of Alabama has a marked history of racism and discrimination. On September 15, 1963, a bomb exploded at the 16th Street Baptist Church in Birmingham, killing four young girls and injuring countless others. This was the pinnacle act of hatred that placed a gruesome exclamation point on a year of racial shift in Alabama's communities.

Just a few months before the bombing, the civil rights movement spilled into the streets of Birmingham. Eugene "Bull" Connor, Birmingham's public safety commissioner, attacked protesters with dogs and firehoses in a stunning scene of racism and horror. In that same year, schools were desegregated in the state, but only after the National Guard was called in to shut down Governor George Wallace's attempt to maintain the racial status quo.

The year 1963 is recent history. For young people, it may seem contemporary to every other historical event they're taught in school: George Washington crossed the Delaware; George Wallace tried to keep schools segregated. The reality is that our society is still filled with those who were alive and present during those dark days of American history. The lightning shift in our racial sensibilities since 1963 is something of a historical wonder. We have since elected a black president and have seen many black Americans rise to the highest roles in society and government. Because of these achievements, many in our country would like to act like all that was done before is atoned for and should be forgotten.

In 1993, I was a fifteen-year-old homeschool kid with pimples—a winning combo on all accounts. I was not unaware of the racial tension that existed in the country or in my community—it just felt distant and incapable of reaching me. The year before, in 1992, the country had watched spellbound as an almost all-white jury acquitted four Los Angeles police officers in the beating of a black man named Rodney King. A witness had caught the beating itself on camera (a precursor to modern America). Even with the overwhelming evidence of injustice, the men were found innocent. The ensuing riots gave a face to the tension that had been boiling in the shadows for decades. Amid the national turmoil, I still felt safe in my white suburban high school existence.

My father was on staff at First Baptist Church in a small town in Alabama, and he was responsible, as is always the case in small churches, for a broad range of things. One of his primary responsibilities was running the church's annual Vacation Bible School (VBS) in the heat of the Alabama summer. VBS was a weeklong event that was part Bible study, part snack time, and part local carnival. This week was a huge outreach to the community, and the church always leveraged the opportunity to encourage new families and faces to join. There was a home in our small town that housed kids who were wards of the state. My father saw this as a perfect opportunity to bring people into our church who may have never heard the gospel. He reached out to the home's leadership and invited the resident children to be a part of VBS that year. Many of the children were black.

Throughout the week of VBS, child after child made professions of faith in Jesus, including several black children from the group home. The Sunday morning after VBS, a handful came down to the front of the church, indicating along with the church's white kids that they had been changed by Christ and wanted to be baptized.

My father was fired from the church that week.

I heard the news of my father's firing on the way to basketball practice at the local recreation center. I was crying bitterly as practice began. My coach—a black man from the community—put his arm around me and told me things would work out in the end. The beauty of a black man consoling a middle-class white kid in small-town Alabama over the ugliness of racism is still not lost on me.

Later in life, I scraped the details together in bits and pieces from my parents. The deacons called Dad into an emergency meeting where he was ordered to "fix" this problem he had created. The deacons rallied around the idea that "no n—er has ever been baptized in our church and never will be." My father refused to bend and was fired immediately.

I had never encountered racism before on such a personal level. The sting of my father's firing was profound. Because we lived in the church parsonage, which literally shared a driveway with the church, we were forced to move immediately. We were graciously taken in by friends who ran a local Baptist conference center and were allowed to live there for the next few months while my family figured out what to do.

It is not an understatement to say that the rest of my life was formed by this experience. While our housing was a godsend, it was also small. I slept on the floor for months. As the eldest of eight children, it fell to me and my brother Bret to work full time to help support the rest of the family in our day-to-day expenses. My father, still bruised from the experience, didn't want to jump right back into a church position, so he took the first job he could find driving an eighteen-wheeler on long hauls coast to coast. We didn't see him for days at a time. Any sense of security that I had been accustomed to was forever replaced with a constant sense of the unknown.

Beyond the physical realities of our new situation, the damage inflicted on my heart burned with the emotional pain of a knife wound. Men I had trusted, men who had taught me in Sunday school, had proved to be the worst of humanity. It is hard for a young heart to process hypocrisy. The stinging reality of racism had pulled back the veil, more than anything, on the darkness of the human heart. For the first time, on an intimate level, I was face-to-face with the worship problem.

As you walk through life, you will encounter the same reality I did as a teenager and continue to encounter as an adult. Perhaps it won't be racism or hypocrisy, but something will allow the worship problem to sink its roots deep into your life through the actions of others. The worship problem touches everything around us. It is the source of every heartache in the world. But there is always hope in the faithfulness of God.

I am now a pastor in a church. I lead the people of God in worship regularly. It is ironic this is who I am now, because after my father was fired in 1993, I swore that I would never work within the church that had hurt me so deeply. Just as the brokenness in the church had reached out and wounded my young heart, Jesus would use the church to reach out and mend it. The church is God's plan to bring us to reconciliation. Worship is our only road back to unity.

In John 4, Jesus meets a woman at a well. It is well documented that he meets her in the heat of the day because she is seeking solitude from those who would deride her for her past sexual indiscretions. He asks her for a drink of water. She asks for clarity on racial divisions. She is a Samaritan; he is a Jew. Perceiving that Jesus is a prophet, she asks him a question about worship and racial tension.

The woman said to him, "Sir, I perceive that you are a prophet. Our fathers worshiped on this mountain, but you say that in Jerusalem is the place where people ought to worship." (John 4:19–20)

Her question is physical in nature. Years of prejudice and distrust between her people and the Jews had led to altercations that frequently ended in physical violence. The Samaritans were the offspring of Jews who had married Gentiles. Half-breeds. Unclean. Unworthy. Less than because of their DNA. This woman associates worship with a place, a people, a culture. She associates worship with division. These are the realities of those who focus on the physical. If the physical is the determining factor in who we are, it will also become the determining factor on where and how we worship and whom we worship alongside. Those who focus on the physical prove that they have not felt the life-giving engine of the Holy Spirit. I love how Jesus answers her physical question with a spiritual reality.

Jesus said to her, "Woman, believe me, the hour is coming when neither on this mountain nor in Jerusalem will you worship the Father. You worship what you do not know; we worship what we know, for salvation is from the Jews. But the hour is coming, and is now here, when the true worshipers will worship the Father in spirit and truth, for the Father is seeking such people to worship him. God is spirit, and those who worship him must worship in spirit and truth." (John 4:21–24)

The physical is temporal. The spiritual is eternal. Worship, fueled by the spirit of God, is the door toward our healing. When people worship God in spirit and truth, the flesh is stripped away. The invitation into the kingdom and into eternity will have nothing to do with skin color or geography. It will not be based on what we have done or our unfaithfulness. When we find ourselves looking at the Father, in eternity, it will be his faithfulness on display. We will be united as one through the power of restored worship in Jesus. We become the answer to the promises made to Abraham so long ago. Paul writes to the church at Galatia:

For as many of you as were baptized into Christ have put on Christ. There is neither Jew nor Greek, there is neither slave nor free, there is no male and female, for you are all one in Christ Jesus. And if you are Christ's, then you are Abraham's offspring, heirs according to promise. (Galatians 3:27–29)

There is a beautiful picture at the end of the book of Revelation. The worship problem has vanished. Eden has returned once and for all.

Then the angel showed me the river of the water of life, bright as crystal, flowing from the throne of God and of the Lamb through the middle of the street of the city; also, on either side of the river, the tree of life with its twelve kinds of fruit, yielding its fruit each month. The leaves of the tree were for the healing of the nations. No longer will there be anything accursed, but the throne of God and of

the Lamb will be in it, and his servants will worship him.
(Revelation 22:1–3)

The Bible ends where it begins, with God's created people worshipping him in a garden. The tree of life has returned. The nations and all their divisions have been healed. Darkness is no more, and God is the center of creation once again. It is toward this hope that we worship in the present. It is with this mission that we seek to be the temple—the connection between heaven and earth—that God has tasked us to become. In the end, the worship problem won't even be a memory. Because of the work of Jesus, we will worship.

Acknowledgements

First and foremost, I would like to give honor and praise to my creator for his kindness and unwavering love. Thank you, Jesus, for giving me the words to write in this book. I pray that they honor you and point others toward your work of redemption.

I would like to thank everyone at Shoreline Church and my friends who serve alongside me there. Jason Hayes, thanks for being a loyal friend and letting me barge into your office to bounce off crazy ideas. Collin, Josh, Corey, Brandon, Holly, Merna, Turner, Henry, Abigail, and Julie, you are the best co-laborers for the gospel anyone could ever hope to have. Chuck, Mark, Jeremy, Brian, Michael, and Matt, thank you for loving me and leading as elders with an undying desire to point others toward Jesus through service.

Huge thanks to all those who have poured into me and my path of worship leadership over the past couple of decades: Joel Brooks, Andy Byers, Michael Adler, Tom Council, Greg Oliver, Gary Greene, Dwayne Waldrep, Tim Kallam, Wayne Splawn, Roger Davis, Wade Morris, Doug Webster, Emily Hooten, and so many more. I would not be who I am today without your kindness.

Finally, I would like to thank my family and friends for their undying support and love. Emily, Lily, Ava, Mae, and Josie, you fill my life with love and joy. Mom and Dad, you bought me that first guitar and set up Mama Camp's piano in the living room. Thanks for leading me to Jesus and showing me what he looks like. Ken and Teresa, you guys are amazing—thanks for letting me marry your daughter! To my seven brothers and sisters, Bret, Micah, David, Libby, Hallie, Elliott, and Zoe, I'm proud to be your big brother.

To the rest of my family whose names cannot all be mentioned here, as well as my church family and countless amazing friends, thank you for your unending love and support. To God be the glory in his church both now and forevermore. Amen.

About the Author

Chuck Hooten is a musician, writer, author, speaker, and pastor from Knoxville, Tennessee. He is husband to Emily and dad to Lily, Ava, Mae, and Josie. Chuck loves reading, adventuring with his family, playing basketball, talking about Jesus, trying new foods, drinking coffee, camping, drinking coffee while camping, and lots of other things. Find out more about Chuck, listen to some music, and drop him a note at www.chuckhooten.com.

Made in USA - Kendallville, IN
1223363_9781735442303
01.11.2021 0814